DAILY EXPRESS
COOKERY BOOK

by
Sheila Hutchins

COLLINS
Glasgow and London

Published by Collins Glasgow and London

First published 1976

Second Impression 1976

Third Impression 1976

Copyright © Beaverbrook Newspapers Limited

Line Decorations by Leonora Box

Printed in Great Britain

ISBN 0 00 435112 6

CONTENTS

PREFACE

You will notice that this book has been metricated at the publisher's urgent request. I don't know if you find it confusing, I certainly do. The metric system is here to stay, however, and we must learn to live with it, although the process of conversion of all our old familiar weights and measures into metric promises to be both painful and complicated.

In an attempt to be helpful and, perhaps, to simplify matters the Metrication Board has already issued a mass of notebooks, pamphlets, short films and leaflets – some in English, others in Welsh – most of them written with all the lucidity of an income tax form. The Board is also taking the process in easy stages so some things are metric and others not. Farmers, for instance, are mostly selling their milk by the litre, though the retail market supplies it in the old familiar pint bottles. Pubs will apparently continue to serve beer in pints and half-pints. Butchers and fishmongers are said to be sticking to the British Imperial measures, though some supermarkets prefer to decimalize their meat and fish.

All change is confusing, of course, and one must learn to adapt; yet when the building trade went metric a couple of years ago one saw nice sensible-looking plumbers near to tears with two lengths of seemingly identical copper piping which didn't fit because one was sent in inches, the other in centimetres.

The metric system works very well on the Continent, of course, and I have a number of cookery books in French and German with the ingredients in metric measures that I find no difficulty in using, having a set of metric weights for the kitchen scales as well as the old ones. It is the business of conversion of existing British recipes into metric quantities that is so confusing. If one tries to convert pounds and ounces, pints, half-pints and quarts into metric measures one gets a lot of nasty fractions which are not only confusing, but unnecessary in the kitchen. The Metrication Board has fixed the 1 oz as equal to 25 grams, which is a good round sum that makes 4 oz or ¼ lb equal to 100 grams. This is very simple and handy but then logically 1 lb is 400 grams. Ah, yes, but it isn't really – because of the odd grams and fractions of grams which have been left out to make a nice round figure, 400 grams is very much less than 1 lb, which is really about 454 grams.

Most British manufacturers and canners, perhaps in fear of contravening the Weights and Measures Act, use this calculation when converting lbs into metric measures and they print it on the tins and packets. I have in front of me one of those familar bags of granulated sugar labelled 2 lb (907 g) in large letters. That makes 453½ grams per lb, doesn't it? If people go by the bag of sugar, however, but weigh out the other ingredients for a recipe at 400 grams per lb as the Metrication Board tells one to do, cakes and puddings will be a disaster.

I feel I should also warn you that if you yourself make a cake entirely using the Metrication Board's suggested conversion to 400 grams and then sell it as weighing 1 lb you might also find yourself in trouble for giving short weight. What is one to do?

The Australians, who went metric fairly painlessly some time ago, have fixed their 1 oz as the equivalent of 30 grams, making 480 grams to the 1 lb, 960 grams for 2 lb – which is only 53 grams different from the one on the sugar bags and many other British manufactured products for that matter. Now it is said that the Metrication Board is thinking of changing its mind and fixing the 1 oz as the equivalent of 30 grams, instead of 25 grams, as the Australians have done.

It is also suggested that they are considering introducing the 'cup system', weighing everything in cups as in the US. This is a dreadful and confusing system as you will know if you have ever tried to use an American cookery book, and of course it is irrelevant in this instance.

All this bother, it is argued, is necessary for uniformity. The whole world is going metric and so we must be the same as everybody else; a reasonable argument, but why does the Metrication Board also say that British cooks should use millilitres when measuring liquids when on the Continent everybody uses centilitres and decilitres instead?

Meanwhile, the people who publish cookery books are very worried, for they have to get the whole thing metricated and sent to the printers months before the book appears. And it is said that school children are already so accustomed to metric measures that the Imperial weights confuse them.

If you are not a school child, however, I should advise you to stick to the good old pints and ounces and so on which you will find in brackets in the text. These are the ones I use myself.

November 1975

Spring

Fascinate your Fishmonger

Fascinate your fishmonger. Get him interested in your little problem. They are – by and large – a fine body of men, anxious to please. For wet fish is not what it was, and trade is dwindling.

What you want is a bag of assorted fish bones and sole and turbot trimmings. For making fish stock, dear, that's what you want them for, and it should be easy enough because no one else is likely to ask for them. They make the most marvellous soup stock which, when cold, will set in a jelly. If you have a really nice fishmonger he will probably give them to you. What you are going to make is a large bowl of scarlet Hungarian fish soup. It's cheap, it's filling and it is delicious.

I avoid the kind of fishmonger with plastic parsley and go, when I can, for the more old-fashioned ones with side whiskers. And a proper fishmonger's hat. Straw boater, madam, surely you've not forgotten. I was talking about curled whiting to one such gentleman only the other day. Know what I mean? Whiting with the tail threaded through the eye socket, the old fashioned curled whiting people used to have. They still serve them like this, egg-and-crumbed, in expensive restaurants but I didn't think anybody curled them in shops now. "Oh madam, could I?" he said rather pathetically. "Do you know, I haven't curled a whiting for years. I would so enjoy it. All the craftsmanship is going out of the business." And he did. And they not only looked pretty but were delicious.

Curled Whiting

Whether curled or plain you dip them in beaten egg and then in a bag of breadcrumbs, patting these on to the fish. You then fry them in hot frothy butter very gently so the fish cooks through before the egg and breadcrumbs get too brown. Take them out of the pan and keep them warm on a hot dish while you heat a little more butter in the pan, add a lemon cut in chunks, peel and all, and some chopped fresh parsley if you can get it. Pour this all hot and frothing over the fish. A glass of light ale with it and the world is yours.

Szegedi Halaszle

As for the Hungarian fish soup, you need 800 g (2 lb) of mixed white fish. A bit of whiting, rock salmon, coley, etc. (In Hungary they use fresh water fish from the river Tisza.) Ask for some fish bones for making the stock. Cut the fish into large chunks, put them on a plate. Sprinkle them with salt and leave them.

Meanwhile fry 2 large finely chopped onions in 25 g (1 oz) of lard till golden. Then, off the heat, stir in 1 level tablespoon of scarlet paprika pepper (but not Cayenne pepper for goodness sake, as this is about ten times more fiery). Stir in the paprika pepper, add the fish bones and 750 ml (1½ pints) of water. Bring this to the boil. Then reduce the heat and let it simmer for 45 minutes with a lid on. Strain it into a clean pan, wipe the salted fish slices, put them in the pan making sure the stock covers them. Cook them slowly with a lid on for another 30 minutes shaking the pan occasionally. Do not stir, this breaks up the fish. Serve it in a hot tureen, with, if you like, a thinly sliced, fresh green paprika pepper (the vegetable not the spice) on top as decoration. You can drink ice-cold lager beer with it.

Spring is the season for sprats too. A curiously neglected little fish which, when crisply fried, is a supper dish for epicures.

Fried Sprats

400 g (1 lb) is ample for two people. Rinse them in cold water, pat them dry in a towel, shake them up in a paper bag with flour, salt and pepper, then fry them in a pan of deep, hot, cooking oil until they go brown and crunchy. They are delicious with a hunk of lemon or a drop of vinegar and a nice plate of bread and butter, or a plate of fresh hot, thickly buttered toast.

They are very good, too, if you dip them whole in a thick pancake batter and then fry them in a pan of hot oil the way sardines are done round the Mediterranean.

The only thing is that both sprats and whiting (unless that's filleted) do have bones in them. The fish itself needs these when at sea in order to lead a fishy life. I do, however, think with all the silly fuss some people make nowadays about fish bones someone would have invented a sort of vacuum cleaner thing to take the bones out of say, a grilled herring as it nestles there cheek by jowl with the mashed potatoes and the mustard sauce on your plate.

But if what you are really looking for is a Boneless Wonder why not try soft herring roes on toast? You can get hard herring roes too but I myself do not like them so well.

Soft Herring Roes on Toast

Toss 400 g (1 lb) of herring roes in seasoned flour. Melt a good table-spoon of butter in a heavy pan, fry them in it gently and when the outside is crisp serve them on slices of buttered toast sprinkled with lemon juice, a little salt and some freshly ground black pepper.

Mussels done with garlic and saffron are delicious cold as starters. And they are boneless too. This is one of those Mediterranean fish dishes which are so fashionable now in some London restaurants.

Mediterranean Mussels

Fry a chopped onion and 2 chopped leeks in 3 tablespoons of olive oil gently in a wide pan with a lid on so they "melt" but do not brown. Add some chopped garlic, 2 chopped tomatoes, pepper, thyme, a bay leaf, 2 glasses white wine and a good pinch of saffron (from good grocers).

Then, having washed 2 quarts of fresh mussels in lots of cold running water, scraped off any sand, seaweed and grit from the shells, pulled off their beards and thrown away any mussels which are broken or remain open, put the rest into the pan, put the lid back, heat fiercely for 2 or 3 minutes. Stir up the mussels so those on top fall nearer the heat and open. When they are all open they are done. Longer cooking will only make them tough. Take them out of their shells, put them in a brown pottery dish, strain the stock over them. Serve them cold for starters.

All these recipes are dead easy and quite delicious. The fish is all cheap and should be quite easy to find. There is only one snag, how-ever, in several places I have mentioned fresh parsley. For some extraordinary reason from about 1st January it disappears from *most* shops and you cannot buy it fresh till early in the following summer. If you ask the greengrocer or fishmonger what has happened to it they say, "it won't grow in the snow, Madam" even if it isn't snowing.

Surely somebody in this country could grow a bit of parsley in a cold frame for the winter months. If not, couldn't we import some during the winter months? We get radishes from America as it is. There is nothing quite like a bit of fresh chopped parsley on top of a plain tomato salad in an oil and vinegar dressing. I could just eat a bit of it now.

I Gotta Loverly Cauliflower

I have a friend who is an impassioned gardener. Last week she produced as a present the largest cauliflower I have ever seen in captivity. It might well have been the Biggest Aspidistra in the World for, with the untrimmed leaves spread out, it was as big as an unfurled umbrella.

The flavour was delicious, all crisp and nutty because it was fresh out of the garden. I staggered into the kitchen with my vegetable trophy and draped it over a plastic bucket, for no vegetable rack would hold it. It was so large you could even have worn it as a hat for the Derby, and since then we've been gorging on cauliflower-and-cheese. Cauliflower with fried breadcrumbs, or toasted almonds. Cauliflower salad, and I have even used the stalky parts for cauliflower soup.

Cauliflower-and-Cheese

I put part of the monstrous vegetable, when boiled, into a small buttery fireproof dish and coated it with old-fashioned egg sauce. Then sprinkled it with grated cheese and browned it in the oven till it was all bubbling.

Cauliflower with Fried Breadcrumbs and Toasted Almonds

Then there was another bit I boiled, and sprinkled with chopped parsley. But also I fried 25 g (1 oz) breadcrumbs in 100 g (4 oz) butter with a handful of skinned, thinly sliced almonds and poured them both over the cauliflower at the last moment. This tastes very good if you can eat it quickly while the butter is still foaming and has not quite soaked into the vegetable.

Cauliflower Salad

If you break the cauliflower into flowerets and just undercook it slightly, it is very nice to eat cold in a homemade salad dressing. I mix two tablespoons of oil to one of mild, or wine, vinegar with a little salt and pepper and rather a lot of garlic powder or crushed garlic. Toss the cooked cauliflower in it. This makes a good salad if garnished with tomatoes.

Cauliflower Soup

The less fascinating parts of the cauliflower can be boiled, puréed in the electric mixer or a food mill. Add salt, pepper, a little grated nutmeg, thin it down with the cooking liquid. Re-heat it and add 2 tablespoons of butter before serving. It makes excellent soup.

And, when you think about it, since a cauliflower is not sold by weight, why in heaven's name do we let them trim it in the shop? For the leaves make quite nice spring greens boiled and eaten with lots of melted butter.

How they Cook in Burgundy

Now it's Spring they must be pruning their vines in Burgundy and covering their dandelions with flower pots. The local snails, too (those famous Burgundian snails who live it up in the vineyards) are waking from their winter sleep, ready to start munching and putting on weight all summer. They should be bulging out of their shells by autumn – which is the time to eat them.

When I was last in Burgundy in November, notices outside vine-yards said "*la chasse à l'escargot est defendu avant le premier Septembre*" – snail hunting is forbidden before 1st September. This is not only to prevent overkill, but to preserve the snail's sex life and plump contented figure – a turgid subject better not discussed. ("Darling . . . let's take off our shells and to hell with it!")

Vineyard snails are large and luscious. The better the vineyard the better the snail tastes. Or is that snobbery? Anyway, I *did* see a snail notice outside the world-famous *Chassagne Montrachet* vineyard.

It was that morning when we drove out to Santenay to taste the new wines from last year's grape harvest. We were with an English Master of Wine who buys burgundy and claret for Harveys of Bristol.

The commune of Santenay consists of nothing but vineyards, a level crossing, rolling country, a small château and one very somnolent railway station in grey concrete with a few plants. No traffic at all. But the wines are world-famous. We took a wine broker or *courtier de campagne*, with us. He lives next door to the château. Traditionally these men keep an eye on the wine when it's racked, see it is sent off properly, arrange payment and currency. There are often friendships of several generations between the *courtiers* and the wine shippers.

Jean Lequin's wines were "still working a bit" and the cellars were heated to hasten the second fermentation. We stood round with our little silver wine-tasting cups while his son climbed up ladders to get samples of new wine out of the vats. Only the real professionals can tell if they will be any good when they are as young as this, and the better the wine will be, the worse it seems to taste. It seems to be almost worse than buying a racehorse and probably just as expensive. When you have rolled the wine round your mouth you spit it out on the floor. I shut my eyes so as to concentrate better. They say in Burgundy you taste the tannin down the centre of the tongue and the acid round the edges. It tasted much worse with my eyes shut, probably because I was able to concentrate better.

"Lot of body," someone said, "almost tingles on the mouth." "Excellent. Excellent." The wine certainly had a slight prickle on the tongue and seemed pale and uninteresting to me, but they said it would be all right after January when it had finished fermenting.

"This one smells of foxes. It will be marvellous . . ." I was glad to spit it on the floor. "It's like 13-year-old girls," Jean Lequin said, "disagreeable. Not pretty – acid in character and still developing." Each tank was different, grapes from different earth or picked on different days. And the experts can taste the wine and tell you whether the sun was shining.

The vineyards are said to be worth £50,000 an acre. Jean Lequin is only a small grower, but the vineyards have been in his family for five generations for certain, and probably much longer. He had about 1,000 dozen bottles in his cellars. The walls were thick with a kind of black fungus which hangs from the walls of all the best wine cellars. It comes from years and years of evaporation of wine through the corks.

We tasted a rare white Santenay that the growers virtually make only for themselves and their friends. "Very beautiful," everyone said. Later Jean Lequin reappeared with an ancient and venerable bottle so thick with dusty cobwebs and the black mould that it appeared to be wearing a fur coat. "This wine is as old as you are, Madame!" he said beaming and offering me the bottle gently, with its long festoons of spiders' webs, on the flat of his two hands. "It was bottled the year that you were born!" "*Ah bon,*" I said briskly, "and what year was that?"

Nobody was prepared to say how old it was, and I doubt if Monsieur Lequin really remembered when it had been bottled. It looked like something that might have been served to Dracula. When I had pulled myself together, however, I realised what a marvellous gift it was – a big, tender, well-matured burgundy, dark, full-bodied and very mellow. We probably have a lot in common. I am going to drink it on my birthday.

As for the dandelions, when young and blanched under a large stone or a brick or a flower-pot, they make the most delicious salad which is served in this part of France with hot bacon fat. And it is not true what children say about them, you can eat dandelions in perfect safety, their French name of *pissenlits* is just a fantasy.

Dandelion Salad

Choose the little leaves just as they come up, cover them for about a week until they are almost as white as celery. Wash the pale stalky leaves, sprinkle them with salt and pepper, a dessertspoon of wine vinegar. Fry 50 g (2 oz) of diced streaky bacon until crunchy, pour the bits of bacon together with the hot bacon fat on to the salad. Stir it up and eat it quickly before the fat sets.

Escargots à la Bourguignonne

You could begin the meal with the famous *escargots à la bourguig-nonne* – snails in garlic butter. These are sold frozen and oven-ready nowadays by most good grocers in Britain.

Allow 6 to 12 per person according to your purse. They are already cooked and you just heat them for about 10 minutes in a moderate oven (180°C, 350°F, Mark 4) until the butter melts. Then eat them with a fork, using hunks of fresh crusty bread to mop up the hot butter.

Boeuf Bourguignon

Here too is the recipe for the famous *boeuf bourguignon* in all its simple majesty as prepared by Edith Remoissenet in the restaurant *Au Petit Truc* at Vignolles, near Beaune, a few miles off.

Take 1 kg (2½ lb) of lean beef, preferably roll of bladebone, cut in chunks. Brown them in a heavy iron pot in 50 g (2 oz) of hot butter a few pieces at a time to colour them well. Take them out and fry two big, peeled, diced onions in the pot with 100 g (4 oz) of pickled pork belly, cut in chunks. When nicely browned, stir in 2 table-spoons of flour, brown that and gradually add two bottles of red wine. Add the beef, a chopped garlic clove, some salt and pepper, two bay leaves, a sprig of thyme and a piece of parsley tied together. Bring it to the boil, put a lid on the pot, let it simmer, bubbling gently, for 2 hours. Thirty minutes before the end, fry 300 g (12 oz) sliced button mushrooms in a little butter. Put them in the pot for the rest of the time. It is generally served with plain boiled potatoes. If you re-heat it, do this gently but not for long.

Ham in Chablis

For this, brown two finely chopped shallots in butter in a frying pan, then add 100 g (4 oz) of sliced button mushrooms, some chopped parsley, and a chopped garlic clove. Put four good thick slices of cooked ham on top and pour a big glass of white wine (preferably Chablis) over them. Let it simmer with a lid on for 5 minutes over a gentle heat, put the ham on a hot dish, let the contents of the pan reduce over heat for some minutes. Add a large tablespoon of thick cream, heat, stirring for a moment. Pour it over the ham. Serve piping hot.

Sausages in White Wine

For sausages cooked in wine, prick 400 g (1 lb) of coarse-cut country pork sausages, put them in a pan with 25 g (1 oz) butter to cook gently for about 10 minutes. Take them out, keep them hot. Stir a tablespoon of flour into the pan, let it brown lightly then gradually add 250 ml (½-pint) of white wine stirring until free of lumps. Add a bunch of mixed herbs, plenty of pepper and put the sausages back in the sauce to simmer for another 5 minutes. Toast some pieces of crisp French bread, lay them in a hot dish with the sausages on top. Strain the sauce over the sausages, eat them at once on hot plates.

Côtés de Boeuf Dijonnaise

For this take 1 k 200 g (3 lb) rib of beef, chined but on the bone, brush it with oil, roll it thickly in dried herbs – thyme, mint, bay leaves, tarragon, fennel, winter savory – and a little salt and pepper. Leave it for 24 hours. Wipe it roughly and brown it rapidly in hot butter on top of the stove. Then roast it in a pre-heated moderate oven (180°C, 350°F, Mark 4) for only 45 minutes. It should be all pink and rare in the middle. Keep it hot elsewhere while you pour 2 tablespoons of warm brandy into the roasting tin, set fire to it then stir in 2 tablespoons Dijon mustard and add 125 ml (¼-pint) stock (bouillon cube). Heat, stirring till the gravy is smooth and thick, pour it over the joint. A superb party dish.

Filled Pancakes

Pancake Batter

The basic British pancake mixture is 100 g (4 oz) of flour and a pinch of salt into which one beats the yolk of one or two eggs; then gradually beats in 250 ml (½-pint) of milk until the mixture is quite free from lumps. Add a little more milk or cold water to make a thin batter. I usually do all this in the electric mixer. Some cooks add stiffly whipped egg white at the last moment, others add a tablespoon of oil when mixing the batter, to make it very smooth.

When you are going to fry your pancakes, only pour enough cooking oil into the pan to make a thin film all over. Get it really hot. Pour in a tablespoon of batter and swoosh it all round to spread all over the pan. I pour the mixture from a kitchen jug which is less messy. When the underneath of the pancake is brown, turn or toss it and fry the other side. You are quite likely to spoil the first one, but what does it matter if nobody is watching? Stir the batter in the jug occasionally, as the flour sinks to the bottom.

Pancakes that are to be stuffed and finished in the hot oven can perfectly well be made in advance. If you hate the idea of Frying Tonight, particularly before visitors, then make your pancakes quietly in the morning and practise alone without embarrassment. Store the good ones stacked flat, sandwiched with foil, one above the other between two plates until supper time. This is what they do in restaurants. You can also make them some days beforehand, wrap them completely in foil and store them in the refrigerator. Or for weeks in the freezer. Heat them up again in a greased pan – or in the oven.

Ham and Cheese Pancakes

I keep thinking about the ham pancakes I had some time ago in a little restaurant at the back of the market in Ajaccio, Corsica, followed by a bit of roast guinea fowl and chips. This was a delicious thing. The pancake, rolled up with a slice of boiled ham and a finger of cheese inside, was put in a metal dish, sprinkled thick with grated cheese, dotted with butter and baked in the oven till the cheese on top was all brown and crisp and toasted while the thick piece of cheese in the middle had melted and was dribbling out of the ends.

Gulyas Pancakes

Left over gulyas makes a perfect pancake filling, as of course does stewed steak and kidney, though I prefer the gulyas. Cut the pieces of meat fairly small and if there is a lot of gravy pour off some to serve piping hot in a little jug. Lay a pancake flat in a round greased fireproof dish to fit it neatly. Sprinkle the pancake with gulyas. Lay another pancake on top then more gulyas until everything is used. The top layer must be pancake. Dot this with butter, sprinkle it with grated cheese. Put it in a moderate oven (180°C, 350°F, Mark 4) until it is all piping hot and the cheese is really toasted on top.

Prawn Pancakes

Peeled prawns or scampi may be mixed with a creamy, well-flavoured white sauce, heated briefly and then sandwiched between the pancakes in the same way. If using frozen scampi or prawns defrost them before stirring them into the sauce. Finish the top with grated cheese, put the dish in a moderate oven (180°C, 350°F, Mark 4) as before, until the whole thing is bubbling and hot. Leaf spinach or grilled mushrooms could be eaten with it.

Pancake Pudding

This is made by filling the pancakes with a mixture very similar to that used for Continental cheesecake.

Mix 200 g (8 oz) of plain curd cheese with 25 g (1 oz) stoned raisins, 50 g (2 oz) sugar, some grated lemon rind, 50 g (2 oz) butter and the yolks of 2 eggs. If using proprietary "cottage" cheese, purée this first in the mixer to reduce it to an even texture.

The pancakes are filled with the mixture, rolled up and stacked side by side in a buttered fireproof dish with a second layer going the other way. Beat up a carton of soured cream with 1 tablespoon of sugar and 1 egg yolk. Pour it over the top. Sprinkle it with a few breadcrumbs and finish the dish in a moderate oven (180°C, 350°F, Mark 4) until thoroughly hot and golden brown on top.

Ox Tongue

Never has it been truer: that old saying about how the woman always pays, especially if she is a housewife with a shopping basket.

If you like food and enjoy cooking, life can be desperately frustrating at present. Everything really cheap seems to have some built-in disadvantage about it, otherwise everybody would have bought it already and the price would have gone up.

Ox-tongue with raisin sauce, however, makes a nice hot family meal that will not cost a fortune. They are surprisingly good value probably because most people don't know how to cook them. They weigh 3–4 lb and are enough for 8–10 people. Smoked tongues are perhaps the most delicious but take longest to cook.

Ox-Tongue with Hot Raisin Sauce

Buy either a smoked tongue or a pickled (salted) one from the butcher and soak it for a couple of hours, or overnight if it has been smoked. Put it in a pan of cold water, bring it to the boil skimming off the froth as it rises. Add 12 peppercorns, 2 bay leaves and some soup vegetables. By this I mean some carrot, turnip, celery, perhaps a bit of parsnip and an onion. Leave the skin on the onion, it gives the stock a good colour and you can use it after for making soup. Let the tongue simmer for about 3 hours or until tender. It is cooked when the tip is soft, prod it with a fork. When it's done trim off any gristle and peel off the outer skin.

It will be absolutely lovely sliced and hot to eat with mashed potatoes and leaf spinach or curly kale chopped with a bit of butter, and the kind of Hot Raisin Sauce which is so popular with ham and tongue both in France and the United States.

Hot Raisin Sauce

For this put 125 ml (¼-pint) of the liquid in which the tongue was cooked into a pan with 100 g (4 oz) of brown sugar, 3 dessertspoons of stoned raisins, the juice of half a lemon and a teaspoonful of butter. Let it simmer gently until the sauce thickens then add the grated rind of the lemon half, and the sauce is ready.

The tongue is delicious cold too. Not just naked and pink as if it had come out of a tin, but with that simple *sauce gribiche* they have in French family restaurants.

Sauce Gribiche for Cold Tongue

For this make an ordinary salad dressing by mixing 4 tablespoons of oil with 2 tablespoons of mild vinegar, or better still, wine vinegar, add a little salt and pepper. Now mash a couple of hard-boiled egg yolks. Stir in the sauce. The egg yolks thicken it slightly. Add a bit of finely chopped raw onion and a few capers. Now, if available, add about 6 little cocktail gherkins sliced in bits, or perhaps some chopped parsley or a bit of finely chopped watercress to make it look interesting.

Slice the left-over cold tongue and pour the sauce over it. Then sprinkle the very finely chopped egg whites on top. It looks most appetizing, and the oil in the dressing prevents any dryness. The sauce is in fact very good on most cold meats.

I don't want to keep on and on, or try to persuade you that merely cooking a pickled tongue will open up a whole new way of life! The stock or cooking water, however, does make excellent soup – if not too salt (which it seldom is nowadays as modern tongues are only lightly pickled).

Garbure

This may not sound wildly exciting but it is in fact a classic – the good household soup, served all over France almost every day in winter, known as *garbure*. You get great steaming white tureens of it with enough for second helpings in most provincial restaurants. With chunks of crusty bread and some good cheese and an apple to follow you don't need much else.

Well I know they don't always make it with tongue stock. Obviously it's a question of what's available, but do try it and be careful not to make it too thick like porridge. French soups are mostly much thinner than those packet affairs popular in Britain. When very thick they don't taste right somehow.

You cut the soup vegetables in tidy pieces and boil up a tablespoon of rice or pearl barley in it. Serve it in a large tureen and garnish it, if liked, with chopped parsley. We generally have a bowl of grated cheese (old stale hard Cheddar grates beautifully) to sprinkle on top of the broth in our soup plates. Slight saltiness in the stock can be corrected by boiling up a good 400 g (1 lb) of peeled, sliced potatoes in it. These absorb the salt and if mashed afterwards will thicken the soup very nicely.

What I do is purée the potatoes and all the other vegetables in the electric mixer with enough stock to make it whizz round properly. Then I re-heat them with more of the stock and I add a lump of butter before serving. The butter is essential for flavour and texture. Just try it. Without it you will merely have *une soupe banale* as the French say.

I am, I must confess, a compulsive soup maker. I put all the left-overs in a pan anyway, usually with some chopped onion and sometimes a bit of garlic too, frizzle them gently in butter then I add water or stock, let it simmer, purée it in the mixer and finish with a knob of butter. You can make very good vegetable soup too quite easily nowadays with the mixer.

Carrot Soup

Ordinary old carrots make a pale orange soup with a delicate nutty flavour. I wash and chop about 400 g (1 lb) of them and let them simmer in a large pan with 2 tablespoons of butter, sometimes with a bit of onion too, for about 15 minutes stirring occasionally. Then I add 2 large potatoes cut in chunks, some salt and pepper and a litre (a good 2 pints) of water and cook it all gently for about 30 minutes. Purée the vegetables in the mixer. Re-heat them in their own stock and pour it all into a hot tureen adding a big tablespoon of butter.

Potage Bonne Femme

A couple of well-washed leeks chopped up with the green and all (gives the soup a nice colour and since you have to pay for it why waste it?) and done in butter with potatoes makes another delicious soup.

Potatoes are marvellous for thickening soup. Less trouble to use than flour, etc., as they don't go lumpy. Soup with potato in it freezes well too.

Celery Soup

Celery can be substituted for the leeks or carrots and makes an excellent soup. I buy a head of "dirty" celery (the kind with earth on it). This not only costs less but has much more flavour than the imported kind in plastic bags and it is easy enough to wash it. Then chop it up, do it in butter and make the soup with a couple of potatoes as before.

A lump of butter or a tablespoon of cream must be added to all these soups before serving but, as a matter of fact, if you have no fresh cream handy the contents of a small tin of evaporated milk goes surprisingly well with most bland soups – better I think than the more costly tinned cream.

Edwardian Fish Pies

The trouble with fish pie is that it must be properly cooked. It is terribly English, though, Edwardian almost. The kind of thing you get in those wildly expensive places where they specialize in poached turbot, grilled herrings with hot mustard sauce, obscure Victorian puddings and very ripe Stilton cheese.

There's fish pie and fish pie, of course. When well-made and properly seasoned as for instance, in some of the London oyster bars, it can be excellent. The sort of food that must have been enjoyed by those Edwardian gentlemen who breakfasted on hock and seltzer water and trained their mustachios with a pair of curling tongs and a lump of moustache wax. Definitely a Man's Dish. Goes with a dozen Whitstable Natives, steamed jam roll, and Guinness laced with champagne.

Some say the best fish pie is made half from smoked fillet, half from fresh. Or from soft herring roes and mushrooms, when it is absolutely superb. I like this too.

Soft Roes and Mushroom Pie

You slice about 150 g (6 oz) of mushrooms and fry them in butter with pepper and nutmeg. No salt – it makes the black juices run out, so add it later.

Shake about 300 g (12 oz) of soft roes in seasoned flour. Fry them in butter, chop them if necessary. Add the mushrooms, stir a spoonful of flour into the buttery juices in the pan and, gently, heating and stirring, add a cup of milk and, if liked, a couple of tablespoons of cooking sherry. Pour it into a pie dish and top it with buttery mashed potatoes, well seasoned with salt and pepper. The potato is especially nice with a little chopped parsley stirred into it. Just before serving put the dish into a moderate oven (180°C, 350°F, Mark 4) to re-heat and brown it on top. It may be served with a tossed salad.

Smoked fillet in white sauce with a good pinch of English mustard powder in it and sliced hard-boiled egg between the layers of fish makes an excellent pie. And what about fresh cod with potted shrimps heated in thin cream? You thicken this with a teaspoon of cornflour and use the shrimp butter, which is most delicately seasoned, to stir into the mashed potatoes.

Old-fashioned Fish Pie

For an old-fashioned fish pie I generally buy coley fillets, which are cheap, full of flavour and you don't notice the slightly off-white colour in the pie when they are cooked. I poach them in milk, using it afterwards for making a white sauce and for the mashed potatoes. Put the fish in a pan of cold milk with seasoning, bring it slowly to the boil and let the fish simmer gently for about 5 minutes, then flake it into a buttered pie dish with sliced hard-boiled egg and chopped parsley. Make a white sauce with the milk, saving a little for the mashed potatoes which you are going to heap on top. Put the pie into a moderate oven (180°C, 350°F, Mark 4) for about 20 minutes to heat through and brown on top.

Fish and Mussel (or Oyster) Pie

Mrs Beeton's fish and oyster pie is "a nice little dish," as she wrote, which "may be made by flaking any cold fish, adding a few oysters, seasoning with pepper and salt, and covering with mashed potatoes: quarter of an hour will bake it."

But oysters were extremely cheap a hundred years ago when she wrote her famous book, and though I do follow her recipe I use a half litre (1 pint) of fresh mussels instead. This is excellent, you get about a dozen.

Wash them in cold water to get rid of any mud, throw away any that remain open or are broken, pull off the whiskers with which they cling to the rocks. Have a hot frying pan on top of the cooker, with a couple of tablespoons of water in it, add the mussels, heat, stirring occasionally for about 5 minutes until all are open. Strain the liquor which comes out of the mussels into a pie dish, add about 400 g (1 lb) of flaked cooked fish and the mussels freed from their shells, throwing away any which have remained closed. Taste for seasoning, add a little pepper, salt, some lumps of butter. Top it with buttery mashed potato and put it all in a hot oven (200°C, 400°F, Mark 6) for about 15 minutes as Mrs Beeton says.

From Point to Point

You do not have to be a racing magnate or even know very much about horses to go to a point-to-point. It is just great fun, a real country outing which doesn't cost much, apart from what you lose on the races, though it would be immeasurably improved by a good picnic lunch.

There are lots of them all over Britain. The jockeys are all amateurs and members of the local hunt, and some of them are women. The farmer lends his fields for the occasion, and, even if it doesn't rain, you will need gumboots, for by the time everybody's been over the soft grass it is like walking through a steak and kidney pudding.

There is a Tote and a few bookies, lots of noise and excitement, people with motor horse-boxes, cars stuck in the mud, tipsters, gipsies, horsy men with bandy legs, tweed caps and heavy-duty agricultural raincoats. If you pay to take your car on the course you can all climb up and sit on the roof so as to see the race properly.

Although there are tents with strong tea, sandwiches and what is often described as cake, lunch is eaten standing round the luggage boot of the car which acts as a sort of table. If it rains you pile into a likely vehicle – a friend's Land-Rover, estate car or something – eating your lunch in a glorious muddle of dogs, gumboots and children. It is difficult at times in the dim light from the steamed-up windows to distinguish between the dog's tail and a hot sausage unless of course you bite it.

In these conditions there is something about a well-chilled bottle of bubbly (whether sparkling white wine or real champagne, if you can afford it) to give the right sense of euphoria. Take ice for it in a vacuum flask. But, since the wind is often cold, take also a vacuum flask of hot soup and mugs to drink it from.

A good, hand-raised, pork pie, cold duck or lamb chops are delicious to eat in the fingers. Cold duck particularly. And some people would not dream of going to the races without rich plum cake or some moist parkin to eat with a hunk of cheese.

If you have one of those zip-up insulated picnic bags which keeps food hot for hours, it will be marvellous. You can fill it with hot Cornish pasties, warm croissants, or Danish pastries, or even hot mince pies laced with whisky.

A really good, hot, Cottage Pie is an absolute winner for a sporting picnic. You can eat it with a fork standing by the car. It goes perfectly with a glass of good claret and, indeed, some gourmets think this simple dish a perfect background to a fine wine. But few people make it properly. A lot depends on the quality of the dripping and the goodness of the meat which must be fresh and well seasoned.

Cottage Pie

You want 800 g (2 lb) of *raw*, lean minced beef. Fry it in beef or bacon dripping. Put it in a pan with a little water and 2 large, peeled chopped onions. Let it simmer as gently as possible for 2 hours, adding salt, pepper and a spoonful of Worcester sauce. Put it in a pie dish. Top it with a purée of freshly-boiled potatoes mashed with butter, some milk or cream, a little salt, pepper, and grated nutmeg and, if you like, chopped parsley. Brown it in the oven.

I do not know why it is so often a dish for using up remains nor why, when you get it in a pub, the meat is so frequently congealed in indifferent gravy.

Saunders

Saunders, a traditional dish still popular in the Midlands, is even easier to take on a picnic for it is completely encased in a brown shiny potato crust.

Season the mashed potatoes with salt, pepper and nutmeg, add plenty of butter. Add enough flour to make a pliable paste. No milk. Use this to line the bottom and sides of a deep, well-buttered cake tin. Fill it with the meat mixture in the previous recipe, though some cooks use finely diced instead of minced beef for Saunders. This too is delicious. Put a roof of the potato pastry 3 cm (a good inch) thick all over. Bake it in a fairly hot oven (190°C, 375°F, Mark 5) till the Saunders is nicely brown and turns out like a cake. Pack it in its tin in your insulated bag. Eat it hot at the picnic with pickles.

A wide-mouthed vacuum flask is perfect for transporting a good Viennese goulash or for Frankfurter sausages in hot water. Eat them with hunks of bread and lots of Continental mustard.

If you have neither, settle for Lancashire hot-pot. The whole thing, jar and all, should be wrapped in foil as soon as it comes out of the oven, then in several thicknesses of newspaper and a blanket. It keeps for several hours in the back of the car and is a classic for sporting events, to eat with pickled red cabbage.

Luscious picnic sandwiches can be made with thinly sliced, smoked cod's roe sprinkled with lemon juice and a little Cayenne pepper, then sandwiched in brown bread and butter. Crisp fried bacon with fried squidgy mushrooms and shredded lettuce makes delicious sandwiches too.

Any further gaps in the picnic basket can be filled with a polythene bag of watercress, some Gorgonzola cheese, black olives and a box of homemade chocolate rum truffles.

Do not forget the coffee and perhaps a flask of something to keep out the cold. There is usually a tent arranged as a bar, though you can seldom get near it between races, for, what with placing bets, looking at the horses, talking to friends, and coming back to sit on the car roof, there is never a spare moment.

But all you really need is to back a winner.

Tarragon

I've got some! I planted it last year and it has come up again beautifully. Tarragon. It is one of those gorgeous cooking herbs that I have always thought difficult to grow (doesn't like the cold or something). Anyhow, I planted it in a fancy pot with a *La France* rose and they must have huddled together and kept each other warm last winter for now both are doing splendidly. Of course you can buy bunches of fresh tarragon from good greengrocers. Some shops and lots of nursery men sell the plant in pots. You can also get it dried – but it is much better fresh. It has an elusive flavour, but then how would you describe the taste of parsley? It is the thing that gives that subtle flavour to the famous French sauces, *Béarnaise*, *Tartare*, *Ravigotte*. You can taste it too in Continental mustard.

Tarragon Butter

But you don't have to be a great sauce cook, for any fool can make a bit of tarragon butter in about two minutes. You just chop it and mix it with a lump of butter then put this – chilled – at the last moment on a bit of grilled salmon or an ordinary grilled steak, or chop, or on a piece of fried fish. As it melts the butter dribbles down all over it and tastes lovely.

Jellied Eggs with Tarragon

If you have any little ramekin or cocotte dishes you are probably as fond of Jellied Eggs as I am, so easy and so pleasant for starters in warm weather. Simply put a poached egg in each pot and fill up with tinned jellying consommé, chill till it sets. The real professional cook's trick, however, which gives the authentic flavour is to add a sprig of tarragon to each little pot with the consommé.

Tarragon Vinegar

You can also make tarragon vinegar for salads by stuffing a bottle with sprigs of tarragon and filling it up with white wine vinegar. It is ready to use in about three weeks.

Tarragon Chicken

When I was staying in Ay, Madame Bollinger, who is head of the famous champagne firm, gave me this recipe for tarragon chicken which is one of the best I have ever tasted. It is unusual as most tarragon chicken recipes tell you to roast it first. This one appears to be popular in the Champagne area as well as in Belgium.

Put a nice plump 1 k 600 g (4 lb) chicken or capon whole into a pan in which it fits neatly. Add a peeled, chopped onion, 1 carrot, 12 peppercorns, a bunch of mixed herbs and some tarragon. Pour in 600 ml (a good pint) of clear white bouillon. It does not matter if this is chicken or beef broth, but it must not be too dark. Bring it to the boil and let the chicken poach gently, simmering until tender in about 45–60 minutes.

Sauce Suprême

Then make a *sauce suprême*. In another pan melt 2 tablespoons of butter, stir in 2 tablespoons of flour and, little by little, add about 375 ml (¾-pint) of the strained chicken liquor whipping it in with a wire whisk and heating till boiling. Let it boil gently, stirring, for about 8 minutes. Beat up 3 egg yolks with 125 ml (¼-pint) double cream in a basin. Gradually whisk in a little of the sauce, then add the rest and heat it gently, stirring, until it is thick enough to leave the trace of the spoon in the sauce. Do not let it boil. Press it through a sieve, stir in a tablespoon of butter, taste for salt and pepper and then add several good pinches of chopped tarragon.

Take the chicken carefully out of the pan, drain it, lay it on a hot dish and cover it with the *sauce suprême*. If you have any fresh tarragon take off a few leaves, plunge them for a moment into boiling water, drain them and arrange them on the chicken as a garnish.

The Pickwick Club

The Pickwick Club set off on its adventures in May 1827 in beautiful Spring-like weather, and I have just been reading about the lovely picnic they all had with Mr. Wardle and the fat boy in an open barouche in Chatham. Fastened up behind it was "a hamper of spacious dimensions – one of those hampers which always wakens in the contemplative mind associations connected with cold fowls, tongues and bottles of wine.

Everybody piled into the carriage, young ladies in scarves and feathers, gentlemen in top boots, and Mr Winkle sitting on the box. After a great many jokes about squeezing the ladies' sleeves, and a vast quantity of blushing at sundry jocose proposals, they all tucked into the cold lobster, pinching the fat boy from time to time to stop him from falling asleep between mouthfuls of veal patty, and to get him to serve out the contents of the hamper." It must have been gorgeous.

The whole book is, of course, full of eating and drinking – brandy and water, bottles of port, boiled tongue and pigeon pies and glasses of East India sherry. From the tea, ham, and muffins with hymn singing, of Mrs Weller, Sen. to her son Sam's dinner of boiled leg of mutton with the Bath footmen. Then there are all the pubs and the accounts of tap rooms from the Bull Inn at Rochester to the Angel at Bury St Edmunds.

Some are real and still flourish, like the Great White Horse in Ipswich, where Mr Pickwick had the shameful encounter with Mrs Bardle in her curl papers. Others are imaginary, like the Peacock at Eatanswill, where the whole Pickwick Club went for the elections. The Leather Bottle at Cobham, where Mr Tracy Tupman regaled his wounded feelings on roast fowl, bacon and ale and etceteras, still serves roast fowl and bacon. The pub is only about five miles outside Rochester, the haunt not only of Mr Alfred Jingle but of Uncle Pumblechook of *Great Expectations*. Nearby Cobham Hall, where Charles Dickens used to stay in a mock Swiss chalet in the grounds, is now a girls' school, but it still has the big laburnum coppice with the yellow flowered trees planted as one might an apple orchard, with carpets of bluebells beneath.

Cold Boiled Beef

If you want some cold boiled beef to take on a picnic ask the butcher for salt silverside, salt topside or the slightly cheaper salt brisket. It should be soaked for about 3 hours in cold water before cooking, or longer depending on how salty it is – the butcher will tell you. Then put it in a pan with cold water. Bring it to the boil, throw away the water, cover it with fresh cold water and re-heat adding 12 peppercorns, a bay leaf, sprig of parsley and an onion stuck with 3 or 4 cloves and let it boil, bubbling away gently to itself till cooked. 400 g (1 lb) will take 1 hour, 800 g – 1 k 200 g (2–3 lb) will take two to three hours' gentle boiling. If it is to be served cold, it should be put in a basin when cooked and covered with its own stock and then have a plate with a weight on it laid on top.

If the stock is not too salty you could use it for fresh minestrone, boiling up a handful of rice with five or six different kinds of sliced vegetables in it. Serve it with grated cheese sprinkled over the top.

Cold, boiled, salt beef goes well with mustard, pickles and horse-radish sauce and salad and makes excellent brown bread sandwiches. You could eat it in some Kentish lane surrounded by fruit orchards, hop gardens and a positive sea of cow parsley stretching from Horsmonden to Dover Castle. "Kent, sir? Everybody knows Kent," as Mr Jingle remarked, "for its apples, cherries, hops and women."

Indeed, some things have changed surprisingly little. Sheep still graze in the apple orchards and I suppose you could still come upon one of those old farmhouses very like the one at Dingley Dell. There Mr Snodgrass stood with his back to the fire sipping his cherry brandy with such heartfelt satisfaction – a large room "with a red brick fire and a capacious chimney, the ceiling garnished with ham sides and bacon and ropes of onions . . .". It is a world of codlin, pies and pippin tarts, tipsy cake and wine jelly.

In those days the farmer's wife and the dairy maids might spend a week preparing for a gathering of relations or the arrival of the Pickwick Club. Cold, jellied fowl, rabbit pie, or hot, pickled belly of pork with fresh-pulled, earthy, new potatoes and tender broad beans in parsley sauce were favourite dishes.

Hot Pickled Pork Belly

You need 1 k (2¼ lb) of very lightly pickled pork belly. Score the skin in 1 cm (½-inch) lines along the grain of the meat. Brush it over with melted lard or cooking oil and put it in a little fireproof dish with 2 tablespoons of water. Bake it in a hot oven (200°C, 400°F, Mark 6) for an hour or until the skin is crisp. Apple sauce is delicious with it.

Battle of the Bulge

I'd eaten so much I'd broken one of my teeth. I had been eating my way through the Ardennes, as a guest of the Belgian Government. Marvellous food, beautifully cooked, with lots of local specialities.

I had tasted poached eggs garnished with hop shoots lightly frizzled in butter, and served with Hollandaise sauce, a dish only eaten for about a fortnight each year when the hops are young. There were chickens cooked with juniper berries, marvellous pâtés and smoked sausages. White wine laced with brandy and flavoured with a sort of wild sorrel from the woods is another Belgian spring-time delicacy.

And believe it or not, in one very distinguished restaurant we began lunch with a delicious *pâté d'anguilles maison* – their speciality, jellied eels flavoured with nettles. "*Mais oui, madame,*" I was told, gravely, "nettles! They also make excellent soup . . ." They don't sting when cooked, incidentally.

The Belgians, who work extremely hard and often have a second job in the evening to make more money, are keen on good food, take an intelligent interest in what they eat, and insist so much on quality that I believe Belgian cooking is now better than in France itself.

In the Ardennes the locally cured hams are not only famous but exquisite, with an aroma and flavour you find nowhere else. They are mostly eaten raw, sliced wafer-thin, like smoked salmon, though they can be cooked. There are two main kinds, one dried, one smoked.

It's a district with vast pine forests full of game, said to shelter 5,000 wild boar – a high rolling plateau with mist in the valleys, grey slate roofs, and pussy willows yellow with bloom. I'd never seen so many sausages. Smoked-cured, garlic and juniper flavoured sausages, black and white puddings, wild boar sausages, pâtés, hogs' head "cheese", roasted sucking pigs and everything.

I'd been up ladders black with tar and smelling of kippers, seen ham after ham hanging in the smoke houses. One small place had over 2,000 being smoked with another 1,000 in the rafters. Huge hams, some weighing over 12 k (30 lb) apiece, for export to Holland.

At Bastogne (where the U.S. and Allied Army may have won the Battle of the Bulge but I certainly didn't), they even select a Ham Queen. In July there's a great Ham Fête and procession, with all the local dignitaries in the gorgeous robes of what I can only translate as The Worshipful Company of Swineherds. The mayor, in ravishing gold and scarlet uniform, is Grand Master of the Order.

Ninety thousand U.S. tourists visit Bastogne every summer and most of them buy a ham. Relatively unknown in Britain, they are beginning to be sold here – though at even higher prices than in Belgium. The pieces of broom and the beech sawdust give it a special taste. Everyone has his own secret mix, though they never use resinous wood such as pine, as it makes your eyes sting and spoils the flavour.

The butchers wear a kind of chain mail vest to prevent injury with the ham knives and I was amazed at the care with which they were boning out even cheap cuts like flank beef.

The Collin family have a small shop and pork-curing business in Bastogne. There was a lovely smoky smell with fresh meat and pies and pâtés in the neatly tiled shop, decorated with antlers, baby wild boars stuffed by a taxidermist, and rows of smoked hams hanging from the ceiling in red and white gingham sacks like shoe bags. In the cellar I met Grandpapa, Monsieur Lucien Collin, quiet and rather shy in his beret and bow tie, patiently rubbing salt and spices into the hams by hand, just as it was done 100 years ago.

Afterwards they pack them in oak casks with herbs and juniper berries and pickle with wood slabs with stones on top to weight them down.

It was Monsieur Lucien's grandfather who started it, and they now send specialities prepared to old country recipes all over Belgium. "A good ham must age slowly like wine," Monsieur Albert Collin told me, as we sat down in the family kitchen to taste the wafer-thin ham with a bottle of Gevrey Chambertin 1966. I met his wife and mother and other members of the family.

It's a proud craftsmanship, sometimes slightly modernized, but mostly full of tradition, though it varies locally. At Florenville, for instance, just by the French frontier, they use different methods from Bastogne, salting the ham with the bone in, sometimes putting cloves in the pickle and not smoking them so highly.

In Bouillon – as in soup – where I spent the night, the pork butcher's shop had a whole smoked wild boar ham, long, lean and with the shiny black hoof still on it which they had smoked specially for a customer. The animal had been shot in the local woods, and breast of wild boar was on sale at 40p per 400 g (1 lb). They also made some into pâté and sell a lot of this in Britain.

Wild boar hams are very dear and tricky to sell as they must be just right, but the shops usually have some for Christmas.

Quails in a Copper Pan

At Grumelange at the *Auberge du Canard Sauvage* – a tiny village inn facing a youth hostel and an ancient, slate-roofed barn – Monsieur Jean Claude Hainaux not only smokes his own hams but cooked us most exquisite stuffed quails for lunch. Two each, served in a copper saucepan sizzling with butter, to eat in the fingers. You can get frozen quails in Britain at varying prices. They would make an exciting dish for a little supper party. First take out the liver and all the red bits from the quails, chop it up with an equal amount of chicken liver and a little lean bacon. Mix well adding salt, pepper, some chopped parsley, powdered bay leaf, a very little garlic and chopped shallot. Then chill the mixture to make it firm enough for stuffing the birds. Thrust a whole bay leaf in each with the stuffing. Then just cook them very gently in a pan for about 20 minutes in butter turning occasionally. He served small finger bowls of cold water for the subsequent mopping-up operation. Messy, but delicious.

Hocks and Moselles

In May, some of the woods and coppices of south Germany are absolutely stiff with wild lilies of the valley, the way ours are with bluebells. The smell is delicious and the carpets of them are so thick under the beech trees that you could sit on them at a picnic. There used to be masses of them, if I remember right, in the woods round Schloss Solitude near Stuttgart and round Marbach where Schiller lived as a boy. The idea, however, of taking a cheap Moselle to the picnic and cooling it in a nearby stream is more romantic than practical. This is the very wine, however, for the merry month of May. It tastes the way you'd think a waterfall would taste, if you know what I mean.

The young beech leaves green as a lettuce, the budding lilac, all seem to be part of it. The wine is delicious with blue trout from a mountain stream, with Rhine salmon, roast chicken and even with clear, strong beef broth with an egg poached in it.

In Germany they often drink them as an apéritif under the lime trees, the scented German *lindenbaum* that you find outside every country inn. For arguably the best wines from the Moselle and the Rhine are really wasted on food – no matter what. They are very subtle and the food is irrelevant. The delicate taste, the acidity, makes it fresh and uncloying even when it is sweet. But they have a powerful perfume, more powerful than any others. A young Moselle as soon as the cork is taken out can sometimes fill the whole room with its scent. It is like a spring meadow with violets, primroses, wild anenomes and woodruff. The blossoms, the spring flowers, you can smell them at once. In south Germany a man is just as likely to have beer with his meal and keep the bottle of good wine to drink under a tree in the evening.

You can find marvellous bottles of Hocks and Moselles in some of the country *gastöffe*, that you never see in England. If you choose one of the very best – and wildly expensive – hocks, a whole pastoral symphony in white wine will be uncorked before you.

But the wine labels are hell. Long stuck together words with no hyphens, printed in Gothic letters . . . terrible! Never before can anything so charming, you say to yourself, have had such appalling long names attached to it, unless it's a garden plant.

German wines mostly come from round the river Rhine or the Moselle. Some of the Moselle vineyards are so steep they seem to go straight up like the roof of a house and workers lay ladders on the ground so as to get up the slope – real cliffhangers.

Rhine wines have been known in Britain for over a hundred years as Hock. A funny name. It is supposed to be short for Hockamore which people say was Queen Victoria's way of pronouncing Hochheimer. These were the wines from a town on the Rhine which she liked to drink so much that they called a vineyard after her – *Hochheimer Koenigin Viktoriaberg*. I think she and Albert used to drink them when they were courting.

Hocks are sold in long slim brown bottles, Moselles in long slim green ones.

The trouble with wine – as somebody once said – is that like sex nobody will admit to not knowing all about it. In Britain masses of people go for *Liebfraumilch* because it has a funny name that most of them can remember. But this is a blend which varies according to who you bought it from. Quite nice, but not necessarily the best buy and not very adventurous. Unless your German is very good, however, it is safer to write down the names than to try and remember them. If you can pronounce it it is probably another blend with a nice easy name thought up for this country. With a bit of patience you can easily unfoozle what it says on the German wine labels. First comes the name of the parish with "-er" stuck on the end (like *Hochheim-er* or *England-er*, meaning, comes from Hochheim or from England). So that *Forster Jesuitengarten* means a wine from the Forst district. This is a very famous Hock. Then there is the name of the vineyard, then the grape, often a *Riesling* – that's just the variety like the Bramley or Granny Smith apples.

Underneath that is a bit about quality. It may say *spätlese*, meaning late picked grapes – it will be very good. Or *auslese*, meaning made from specially selected grapes – even better and more expensive. Then there is *beerenauslese*, selected single grapes picked one by one from the very ripest bunches – this will be sweet and luscious and even more expensive. Then there is *trockenbeerenauslese*, made from individual selected grapes when they have dried and shrivelled up so they look like raisins. Madly expensive.

This is really like the dogs in the fairy tale, the first with its eyes as big as saucers, the second with its eyes as big as cartwheels and the third with eyes as big as church spires.

Piesporter Goldtröpfchen is a world-famous Moselle wine, very pale in colour, delicate but not flowery. *Bernkastler Doktor* and *Bernkastler Schwanen* are two more world-famous wines, very pale with a slightly flowery, almost nutty, taste to them. The *Johannisberger* wines are very famous Hocks, sweet, soft and yellow in colour. *Rüdesheimer* wines are equally well known and would be perfect at a dinner party when you were trying to impress. But really it is up to you. Settle down with a good wine merchant's catalogue and work it out for yourself.

Blue Trout

Blau Gesottenne Forelle is perfect with white wine. The skin of an absolutely fresh trout goes bright blue when the fish is poached in vinegar and water. It tastes delicious but chefs always say it must be killed just before cooking or it won't go blue. Fritz Michels of the Schaumbergerhof Hotel, Bonn, once told me that deep frozen trout can be done like this too if, after thawing, the skin is still sticky all

over with the slime you find on a live trout. This makes it go blue.
Have ready a shallow pan of ⅔ salted water and ⅓ vinegar rapidly
boiling. Don't scale the fish, clean it on a wet kitchen board, salt it
on the inside only for fear of damaging the sticky slime. Plunge
them in the vinegary water. Medium 125–175 g (5–7 oz) trout take
about 5 minutes to cook. Drain. Serve with parsley, hunks of lemon,
plain boiled potatoes and a jug of melted butter. I cannot get the
deep frozen ones to go very blue myself but they are still delicious
and make a perfect and delicate little supper dish. Mackerel can also
be cooked like this.

Potato Dumplings

Potato dumplings as light as a cloud are a speciality of the Rhine-
land. I had them with saddle of venison and cranberry sauce but they
are equally good with casserole chicken, jugged hare or even English
steak and kidney. To make them, press some cold boiled potato
through a sieve adding a little pepper. Beat in a broken egg to bind
it. Form the mixture with your hands into tiny dumplings. Poach
these in boiling salted water for 18–20 minutes.

German pastry cooks are said in the trade to be the best in Europe
and even the smallest town has two or three first-rate cake shops
full of rich and improbable cream cakes all made on the premises.
That mouthwatering baked German cheesecake sold in English
coffee shops is made from unsalted curd cheese. German housewives
always complain that when made at home the cake goes soggy in
the middle. Herr Christian Dreesen, a master pastry cook from the
Poststrasse in Bonn, gave me two wonderful tips for making perfect
cheesecake.

Baked German Cheesecake

Grease a 22 cm (9-inch) loose-bottomed cake tin or spring form,
line it with flan pastry (200 g [8 oz] plain flour, 100 g [4 oz] butter,
1 tablespoon sugar, mixed with an egg instead of water). Prick the
bottom with a fork, bake it for about 15 minutes in a moderate oven
(180°C, 350°F, Mark 4).
Herr Dreesen says no stones, dried beans nor rice are necessary to

weight down the empty pastry case as most cooks think, including myself, if, when the pastry begins to rise in the middle you just take it out, prick it again and put it back to finish cooking. And do you know, he's right.

For the filling, press 600 g (1½ lb) unsalted curd cheese through a sieve with the grated rind of a lemon, a good pinch of salt and 40 g (1½ oz) cornflour. Slowly beat in 250 ml (½-pint) of stiffly whipped double cream, then, having beaten 4 eggs with 150 g (6 oz) of sugar fold them into the cheese mixture, not the other way round. Fill the cold cooked pastry case with it, bake it 25 minutes in a moderate oven (180°C, 350°F, Mark 4). As the middle begins to rise take the cake out for 10 minutes to cool, put it back in the oven. Repeat, baking it three times altogether for a total of 60 minutes. Loosen the pastry from the sides of the tin but leave it in it to cool. Herr Dreesen says if you add stoned raisins put them on the bottom as they make the mixture soggy.

There is also a gorgeous, uncooked German cheesecake, even better I think than the other, which has suddenly become fashionable.

Though very rich it is not sickly and quite easy to make. I have extracted the recipe for you from the Café Nick, an elegant little shop with only three tables usually full of diplomats' wives, in the Tannen Allee, Bad Godesberg. Among their specialities was a hazelnut cake shaped like a huge daisy and decorated with tiny Japanese parasols.

Uncooked German Cheesecake

Sieve 200 g (8 oz) of unsalted curd cheese, beat it up with 50 g (2 oz) of caster sugar and the strained juice of half a lemon. Add 250 ml (½-pint) of stiffly whipped double cream and then strain in 6 g (¼-oz) of powdered gelatine melted in a couple of tablespoons of hot water and allowed to cool. Beat the mixture well. Put the bottom of a 15 cm (6-inch) sponge sandwich cake in a deep 15 cm (6-inch) cake tin, lined with foil or greaseproof paper. Heap the cream mixture on top of it, it will be 5–7 cm (2–3 inches) deep. Lay the other half of the sponge sandwich on top, sprinkle thickly with caster or icing sugar and chill for at least 2 hours before serving it. You can easily get it out of the tin with the help of the foil lining.

Summer

Eggs

In this permissive age when most folks have got rid of their silly superstitions about sex, you would think they would be a bit less knotted about eating as well. Yet some people still believe that eating raw vegetables will give them worms and that munching watercress, even if they wash it well, will cause tadpoles to form and swim inside them (must be terribly ticklish). There are people who believe that if you so much as swallow some chewing gum it will wrap itself round your heart and squeeze you to death and that if you drink whisky after eating grapes you will hiccup for a week.

They also believe that boiled egg water gives you warts, and that if you eat bananas when you are expecting you will have a bow-legged baby. Of course we are still living in a haunted, hag-ridden, superstitious world and though I have always known there were a lot of extraordinary ideas about food, the more I think about it the more I realize that if they were all true we'd be a desperately hungry lot.

You can still find people who will tell you never to swallow apple pips for fear of having a fruit tree growing out of one ear, and most fruit and nearly all green vegetables were once suspected by someone somewhere.

And: "If you sit on the cold stone," they said when I was a child, "it'll strike up." You will be relieved to hear that it never did.

It was at about this period that I made friends with a hen. She used to stare at me with her head on one side then suddenly blink, letting down her bald, featherless eyelids like roller-blinds and striding off into the nesting box to lay something lovely for tea. Her name was Martha. Have you ever known a hen well? They are not, it must be admitted, very intellectual or rewarding companions, but in my solitary rural childhood my choice was limited.

There is of course nothing quite like a large, brown, absolutely fresh egg. The kind laid by a hen that scratches about in the farmyard and who chortles with pride in her achievement before walking to her habitual dust bath at the back of the wood shed.

Indeed, some of my best friends have been hens, as the saying goes.

I mean, think of a huge fragrant mound of buttery scrambled eggs, bright yellow and all runny in the middle, filled with fresh boiled garden asparagus and garnished with watercress (tadpoles and all!). I had some of this for lunch yesterday and the cress was still crisp and all pepper-tasting when I ate it. The whole thing took about four minutes from start to finish. Served in my mother's old Sheffield plate entrée dish it makes an elegant first course, too, for a little luncheon party.

Pickled Eggs

And do you remember those pickled eggs people used to have in country pubs? Simply hard-boil the eggs, then drop them in cold water and shell them. Put them in a wide-topped jar with a few bay leaves and some little red pickling chillis, if you can find them. This is partly for the look of the thing. Fill the jar with enough cold, spiced vinegar to cover the eggs well and put the top on. They will be ready to eat in two days' time.

For the spiced vinegar, add 12 g (½-oz) each of cloves, peppercorns, and stick of cinnamon, a piece of nutmeg and a little bit of whole bruised ginger to 1 litre (2 pints) of vinegar. Cover the basin and stand it in a pan of hot water. Bring to the boil then take the pan off the heat. Just leave the spices in the warm vinegar for about 2 hours before it is used.

Eggs in Onion Sauce

Sometimes I cook eggs in onion sauce in individual white pottery dishes, rather like coffee cups with no handles. I have a whole set of these, which I found in a second-hand shop in Hastings some years ago.

I saw them out of the corner of my eye as we were driving past. They were stuck out on a table in front beside some old electric kettles, a broken down ironing board and some mud-coloured chairs. There was a whole tray of cheap oddments with these little pots and some lovely white meat dishes that the man said had come from the local French convent which was modernizing its equipment. Modernizing! You can get something similar from big stores nowadays but they won't be as cheap as mine were.

For the eggs in onion sauce, boil them a bit longer than if you were eating them in their shells for tea. The yolks should be soft but the whites firm enough for you to peel the egg without bursting it open. Put 6 eggs in a pan, pour on boiling water to cover and allow five minutes from the time the water comes back to the boil. Take them out, put them in cold water for a few minutes. Peel them very carefully, rinsing off any bits of shell sticking to them.

Meanwhile cook 200 g (8 oz) of peeled, sliced onions gently in 40 g (1½ oz) of butter for 7 or 8 minutes with a lid on the pan so they melt rather than brown. Stir them occasionally. Then stir in a dessert-spoon of flour, a pinch of nutmeg, some salt and pepper, and gradually add 250 ml (a scant ½-pint) of milk, stirring.

Heat, gently, stirring occasionally, till the sauce is smooth and thick. Put the boiled eggs in a buttery ovenproof dish, pour the sauce over them, sprinkle the top with grated cheese and put them in a hot oven (200°C, 400°F, Mark 6) just long enough to brown the top.

Little Pots of Chocolate Cream

I use them for little pots of chocolate cream, another old favourite which was known as Chocolate Pots in my childhood. Beat up 3 egg yolks with 50 g (2 oz) of sugar and stir in 125 ml (¼-pint) of cream. This could be out of a tin if need be. Melt 100 g (4 oz) of plain bitter chocolate gently in 125 ml (¼-pint) of milk, stirring all the time. Add a teaspoon of instant coffee powder, a teaspoon of butter, stir it into the egg mixture. Pour into the pots. Stand them in a baking dish with hot water to come just over half way up. Put a sheet of foil on top, cook them for about 20 minutes in a moderate oven (180°C, 350°F, Mark 4). Delicious when served cold.

Fritto Misto Mare

One of the most delicious things, I think, for supper is crisp fried squid or cuttlefish such as you get in the little shops in the back streets of Venice as part of a *fritto misto mare*, which is just the Italian name for mixed fried fish.

Fried Squid

Squids are relatively inexpensive and on sale nowadays in the more enterprising British fish shops. Vast quantities of them are caught in the English Channel off Dungeness. They are the things with little tentacles and a bag like a small hot water bottle at the back.

Chop off the tentacles, pull out the little bone like a bit of transparent plastic and chop off the bag part, but be careful not to cut up the little ink sacks in front as they are rather messy. Cut all the rest in strips. There is no need to make any batter. Have, say, an old soup plate with half a cup of flour in it and another containing two eggs beaten up with a pinch of salt. Dip the bits of cuttlefish or squid in first the flour and then the beaten egg. Fry them in your pan of very hot oil. They are done when brown all over, do not cook them more than 5 minutes.

Pieces of hake or other white fish cut in fingers can be fried in the same way, as can scampi or prawns but if frozen let them thaw first. In Venice they also include tiny red mullet and fresh cooked mussels, dipped in flour and egg and fried, in a *fritto misto mare*. There used to be a restaurant on the edge of a rather decrepit looking pier or harbour mole in the old part of Rimini where they did it beautifully. Thinly sliced baby marrows or zucchini can be dipped in flour and egg and fried and included in the *fritto misto*.

Fried Whitebait

Whitebait – baby herrings and sprats not much bigger than matchsticks – are a great delicacy and are cooked a bit differently: no egging. The trick is to wash them in chilled salt water, pat them dry in a tea towel, and shake *a few at a time* in a paper bag of seasoned flour. Fry them at once in the hot oil *a few at a time*. They only take a couple of minutes to cook, but too many will cool the cooking oil and if you keep them waiting they go damp and the soggy flour makes them stick together. Eat them at once, whole and still crisp. You eat the whole thing, heads, tails, bones, everything and the smaller they are the more they are prized. King Edward VII was mad about them. 200 g (8 oz) per person makes a substantial main course and less if they are for starters. Serve lemon wedges, black pepper, and thin brown bread and butter.

And here is a bit of wisdom about deep frying. Always dry moist food, especially chips, to reduce the "foaming" when they go into the hot oil. Lower the food in gently, and if you are using a frying basket be ready to lift it if the "foaming" rises too high in the pan. If the things are not completely covered turn them with a skimming ladle or fish slice, otherwise leave them alone. Fish them out when crisp and brown and drain them on a sieve. Do not use a lid for deep frying. Do not leave the oil unattended while heating if called away. Switch off. And when frying is finished turn off the heat. If any oil spills over and catches fire, put it out by smothering with salt, *not water*. When cool, drain the oil straight into a jar through a sieve to get rid of any gubbins in it. You can use it for fish again and it keeps quite a long time if used fairly regularly.

Bantry Races

The Bantry Races is a 25-year-old annual event in a big sloping field with a trout stream at the far end near the fish and chip van. When I was there there were a lot of horsy looking men in navy blue suits with brown felt hats, but there were only three runners in the 2.30, which started somewhere around 3.20, some of the contestants having been unavoidably delayed and arriving very late. I saw no less than eight horses getting out of one cattle truck. People were rubbing them down with wisps of hay and one horse box, which looked rather like a bright verdigris-green, inverted bath tub, had a horse kicking it to hell inside.

Buttered Eggs

We sat up on the hillside eating a lovely Irish picnic lunch. Fresh brown soda bread, yellow creamery butter, cold boiled bacon and buttered eggs. These are a local speciality with an indefinable flavour and are equally good boiled or fried with rashers. You take the eggs fresh from the nest, wipe them lightly if stained but don't wash them. Smear your hands with butter and cover each egg completely in a thin coating of it. Store them pointed end down in an egg carton. The butter not only preserves them but flavours the eggs which are usually free-range in Ireland where they give them raw to race horses to improve their coats.

By now the jockeys were already weighing-in in the paddock on what appeared to be a pair of kitchen or bathroom scales balanced, for steadiness, on a strip of broken hardboard set firmly in the long grass – though I believe this was modified later. Several women in black knitted shawls were selling religious emblems and telling you how you had a lucky face, but though I asked one of them who was going to win the West Cork Derby she wouldn't be drawn and pointed out that the bookies, on most races, were only giving even money on the field.

The jockeys all looked like children to me riding in race after race. One was a girl apparently about thirteen "though well developed" as all the men said. Another was a small boy who didn't seem to have enough leg on him for the big horses and fell off in the last race. The doctor in our party responded to the emergency help call but said afterwards it was apparently just light concussion. He was amazed, though, to find himself elbowed out of the way "by various elderly ladies who breathed into the child's ear" and seemed to be saying the good word and breathing life into him. Nobody I met in Ireland was in the least surprised by it.

Afterwards we went round to a nearby hostelry for a drop of the hard stuff. Himself was standing behind the bar in his bare feet, but wearing a monocle, and was kind enough to offer us some of his ten-year-old Jack Rearden whiskey.

We dined on his wife's clear mussel soup, thick with onions and parsley, and on Bantry Bay scallops cooked in cream and whiskey. "You're a woman after my own heart, Sheila," he said to me laughing, "both you and my wife Audrey do their hair so that it looks exactly like an old lavatory brush." The rest is silence.

We had driven over from Ballydehob, a pretty village on Roaring Water Bay about 15 miles off. It's at the head of a long creek with an abandoned viaduct once used by the Skibbereen and Skull Light Tramway which closed about thirty years ago. You still see abandoned tram cars on the moors used as sheep shelters and summer houses.

There are old oyster beds too in Roaring Water Bay that nobody bothers with now, only the conger eels eat them.

Rabbit Stew

One night, some members of the party having been out rabbit shooting, we had bacon and rabbit stew in thick parsley sauce, and potatoes boiled in their skins to eat on side plates with butter. Then there was gooseberry pie with a mug of thick yellow unpasteurized cream from a place down the road and we washed it all down with glasses of Paddy.

For the stew, cut up the rabbit and leave it to soak for about an hour in cold, salted water with a dash of vinegar in it. Then wipe the rabbit pieces, put a couple of peeled sliced onions in the pot with six bacon rashers (or one of those Irish "bacon ends" they sell in the Skibbereen shops) and the rabbit pieces. Add more sliced onion, one or two chopped carrots, some pepper and parsley with water almost to cover, and a lid. Put it in a moderate oven (180°C, 350°F, Mark 4) for about 1½ hours till the meat is dropping off the bones. Pile it up on a meat dish and pour thick parsley sauce, made with the rabbit stock, over it. Lovely.

Round here the cows stand deep in grass tussocks, there are arum lilies before the cottages and in the marshy places huge wild purple orchids, yellow flag iris and white bog cotton. The cottage doors are always open, everyone greets you, knows who you are and mostly where you've been as well. Great "cakes" of soda bread stand on the table at tea time made fresh every day in Irish farmhouses where the word "bread" is used scornfully to describe an ordinary factory loaf.

Soda Bread

Mix 400 g (1 lb) of plain stone-ground wholemeal or whole wheat flour (such as Allinson's) with 200 g (8 oz) of plain white flour, 2 teaspoons of salt and 2 teaspoons of baking soda. Make a well in the middle. Gradually stir in about 375 ml (¾-pint) of fresh milk, butter-milk or sour milk using a wooden spoon to make a soft manageable dough. The exact quantity of liquid depends a bit on the quality of the flour. Knead it in the mixing bowl with floured hands into a round ball. Flop it on to a lightly floured baking sheet, flatten it with your hand into a 4 cm (1½-inch) thick round. With a floured knife make a cross through the middle "to let the devil out". Bake it at once in a really hot oven (220°C, 425°F, Mark 7) for 25 minutes then reduce the heat to moderate (180°C, 350°F, Mark 4) for another quarter of an hour. Leave the bread standing upright to cool and don't cut it for several hours till it has set.

Mint Tea and all that

Cool, they say, as a cucumber . . . And this is the weather to sit under a tree in the deep peace of some English garden and eat thin cucumber sandwiches. And to drink long, cool draughts of mint tea. This is made twice as strong as usual and served cold with sugar, but no milk, in a tall glass with chunks of ice and a sprig of mint and a slice of lemon.

As the sun veers round and begins to sizzle on the sun tan oil, I long for a huge, cool drink of homemade barley water, or my favourite fruit drink which is just the juice of a huge fresh lemon squeezed into a tumbler with cracked ice, caster sugar and a lot of soda water. One of the coolest imaginable drinks is just strong cold tea with lemon juice and a dash of rum let down with a third soda water or other fizzy mineral. Pour this into a screw-topped bottle and leave it for a couple of hours on ice. It is perfect to take out and leave under a tree when hay making.

If you have been in the country sniffing the delicious grape-like odour of the elderberry flower (these are the huge white clusters of bloom that village children in some parts call "bread and cheese") which are now thick in the hedgerows you will want to make elderflower bubbly. It is a delightful summer drink which foams deliciously when done, but it is not intoxicating.

I remember sipping it on a hot June afternoon three or four years ago when visiting Mrs Appleby who lives in a pretty cottage in Grassington, Yorkshire and is an authority on local dishes.

Elderflower Bubbly

Simply put 600 g (1½ lb) of sugar, 2 tablespoons of white wine vinegar or white distilled vinegar in a very large bowl with four big heads of elderflowers and 4 litres (1 gallon) of cold water. Squeeze, quarter and add two lemons. Let it stand for 24 hours, stirring occasionally, before straining and bottling it in screw-topped bottles. It is usually ready to drink after a few days but sometimes takes a couple of weeks to become a bubbly drink depending on the weather and so on. Recork it if it is not ready. It will keep for months and I have kept mine in a cool cellar for over a year. It is a nice, cool, slightly sparkling drink which is very good iced to add to gin instead of tonic water. Perfect for hot summer days, it is cheap and simple to make and also just the thing for hay making.

The deep peace and silence of the summer afternoon in our garden is disturbed, I may say, by the perpetual, worried chink-chinking of a pair of blackbirds whose fledglings have just left the nest and seem to be in constant peril from an errant tabby cat. "Quick-quick," they seem to say, "Quick-quick, it's after our Jimmy . . . quick-quick." Jimmy is all fluffed up and has no tail and just sits in the top of a bit of privet waiting for the next worm and too frightened to fly back.

While we are waiting I will give you my recipe for Victorian barley water. This is nice chilled and served in an old-fashioned bedroom wash jug, if possible with some ice cubes to tinkle frostily in the glass.

Barley Water

Wash 50 g (2 oz) of pearl barley in cold water then put it in a pan with 500 ml (1 pint) of cold water, bring it to the boil and boil it for 15 minutes. Strain off the water and throw this away. Now pour 2 litres (4 pints) of fresh boiling water on to the pearl barley and boil it until reduced by half. Meanwhile put the peel of two lemons with 25 g (1 oz) of sugar and 500 ml (1 pint) of cold water in another pan and heat gradually, stirring until the sugar melts. Bring it to the boil and simmer till it tastes of lemon. Add the lemon juice. Strain it and pour it into the barley water. Chill.

I think Jimmy will make it. He is now sitting on the gate post huddled, as it were, in his winter woollies but obviously just about to take off.

Strawberry Sandwiches

The best sandwiches for tea under the trees are the kind they used to make on farms and in English country houses when the soft fruit was in season. You just pick a few ripe strawberries in the kitchen garden, roll them in caster sugar, mash them to a pulp and spread this thick on fresh bread and butter to make the sandwiches. Do not use too much of the juice, it makes the bread soggy. Save it to stir into a strawberry fool. Raspberries or red or white currants or squishy purple mulberries are equally good for this.

Raspberry Jam

People often ask me if I have a recipe for uncooked raspberry jam. It is a very simple one, and although it will not keep very long, it tastes deliciously of fresh, warm summer raspberries.

You need two fireproof, glass, pudding basins. Put 800 g (2 lb) of raspberries in one and 800 g (2 lb) of granulated sugar in the other. then stand them in a moderate oven (180°C, 350°F, Mark 4) for about half an hour so they get really hot, but don't allow them to boil.

Mix the fruit and the sugar together in a large basin, stirring with a wooden spoon until the sugar has quite melted and is well mixed with the fruit.

Now pack it in warm jam jars and seal. Even in the fridge it won't keep for very long but I expect you will have eaten it before then.

Vitello Tonnato

Vitello Tonnato is the kind of thing you find proudly and prettily displayed among the little wild strawberries, the mounds of cold asparagus in mayonnaise and the bottles of Chianti in small dark, but cool, family restaurants all over Italy. They have huge fancy platters of it garnished deliciously with black olives, sliced lemon and a lot of capers. It is very rich but beautifully cool and refreshing. Consisting, in fact, of thin slices of cold cooked veal in tunny fish mayonnaise. It is not half so mad as it sounds. I make it, not with veal, but with cold chicken or turkey. Perfect for a festive meal.

The cooked chicken or turkey must be sliced nicely without the skin and bones and laid on a platter, then covered with a special sauce, the day before if possible so it can absorb the flavour. To make the sauce I put the juice of a lemon and one large egg yolk into the electric mixer with the contents of a small tin of tunny fish in oil, previously mashed lightly with a fork. I add a breakfast cup of olive oil, a little salt and pepper, switch on and let the whole thing whirl round until it goes smooth and thick like ordinary salad cream or mayonnaise. Keep cool, don't panic, it sometimes takes two or three minutes to thicken. You can add one or two tablespoons of double cream at the last moment, if liked, before spreading it smoothly over the chicken or turkey pieces. If it is very thick, however, let it down with just a little more lemon juice. Before serving make a border to the dish with sliced lemon, cold new potatoes tossed in parsley and a little oil (not butter it sets solid), some fluffed-up mustard and cress or little bunches of watercress. Sprinkle some well-drained capers on top.

A Sumptuous Meal

The sun was so hot it melted the butter on my plate at lunch. The light here is different I kept saying to myself, and everything's dark green with almost porridge coloured, but sometimes red, earth – burnt umber I think they call it. It would be marvellous to come here after a nervous breakdown or something or with your lover – preferably a millionaire father-figure – for an extremely sophisticated week-end. But if you were 17 and arrived with Mummy you'd go raving mad.

I was staying at Oustaù de Baumanière, a small quiet hotel up in the hills 80 kilometres (50 miles) north of Marseilles. It's got vaulted stone ceilings, a faint wind rustling in the willow trees and one of the twelve best restaurants in France. The menu is quite short but absolutely breath-taking. Locally they specialize in asparagus, new potatoes and strawberries. The rich soil of the Rhone valley is ideal for market gardening and you see little fields like kitchen gardens sheltering from the sun behind tall cypress hedges.

Whilst I was eating my roast lamb and *gratin dauphinoise*, the waiter brought me some little, purple, globe artichokes, no bigger than hen's eggs, which he had grown in his own garden. You eat them raw. He pulled off the outer leaves and told me to dip them in the gravy. They smelt like newly-mown hay and tasted like fresh Kentish cobnuts. There are some fantastic ancient bottles in the wine cellar you'd probably find nowhere else on earth.

The village, about 1½ kilometres (1 mile) up the road, is really an old ruined city where they used to quarry stone. Most of the original inhabitants have gone and it now looks like a film set but it gives its name to bauxite, a mineral discovered here in 1922 from which comes the modern aluminium industry.

The kitchen is not, after all, so very grand for such a place I said to myself, it's their attention to detail that is the making of it. I hesitated for a long time over the marvellous cheese and their famous pancakes filled with orange soufflé. There was a bowl full of marrons glacés, Château d'Yquem 1921 and all that. But in the end I just had a few garden strawberries without cream or anything and felt at peace with the world.

For their famous *Gigot d'Agneau en Croûte* (leg of spring lamb in puff pastry) the legs weigh less than a kilo (2 lb) and come from local spring lambs from the Massif Central. Each is numbered. Mine was 56143. They bone them as far as the shank, which is left in like a kind of handle, then stuff them with kidneys and cook them in pastry.

Gigot d'Agneau en Croûte

Fry 3 diced lambs' kidneys in 40 g (1½ oz) of butter for about 3 minutes. Stir in a little Armagnac brandy, some chopped mushroom, thyme, rosemary and tarragon. Use this to stuff the meat. Sew it up with kitchen thread. Brush with melted butter. Put it in a very hot oven (230°C, 450°F, Mark 8) for 15–20 minutes just to stiffen the meat. Remove. Let it cool while you roll out enough puff pastry, 1 cm (½-inch) thick, to cover the joint completely. Moisten the edges, pinch it together with your fingers. Brush with egg yolk. Put it back in the oven to finish cooking for 15–20 minutes. Frenchmen like their lamb cooked very rare, but it should be left a little longer in England.

Gratin Dauphinoise

With it they served a *gratin dauphinoise* which I think is one of my favourite potato dishes. My recipe, which follows, is slightly less rich than theirs which is cooked with thick cream. If liked, cream could be substituted for the second amount of milk. It is very good, very rich.

Peel and cut 800 g (2 lb) of potatoes in thick rounds. Put them in a pan of well-seasoned, boiling milk and let them simmer till half cooked. Rub a bit of garlic round a wide shallow fireproof dish. Beat up 2 eggs with 100 g (4 oz) of grated cheese. Pour in 375 ml (¾-pint) of hot milk, add the potatoes. Tip it all into your fireproof dish, top with another layer of grated cheese. Brown in a moderate oven (180°C, 350°F, Mark 4) for 30–35 minutes.

Floating Dessert Islands

Raspberries and strawberries are at their best with icing sugar. I don't know why, but if you once try it, you will see that this is so. One wants something cool and summery to have with them. So I have been reviving my Floating Islands, cold and pale, and with a scent and flavour like warm sun-kissed glass houses full of grapes, they go perfectly with the soft fruit.

All round the Mediterranean they make luscious sweet white wines from *muscat* or *moscato* grapes. Some of the wines have an almost overpowering scent and this strange, musk-like flavour which comes from the grapes themselves. Know what I mean? It's like over-ripe melons or crushed geranium leaves which sometimes have an even stronger muscat smell than grapes do, and the plant is even called *Muscatli* in Hungary, probably because of the way it smells.

Floating Dessert Islands

But how to reproduce it in a pudding? Well I simply simmer 3 or 4 well-washed geranium leaves in the milk of the Floating Islands–you will see how in a minute. Whip the whites of 4 eggs so stiff the basin may be turned upside down without them falling out. Stir in a teaspoon of sugar. Heat 500 ml (1 pint) of milk gently in an absolutely clean frying pan. Lift out lumps of whipped egg white, a tablespoon at a time, and tip them into the milk to poach. Turn them over with a slotted spoon or fish slice after 2 minutes. Leave them another minute (no longer or they collapse). Fish them out, put them on a clean, spread-out tea towel to drain. When all are done, put your geranium leaves into the milk and let it simmer gently for 5 or 6 minutes. At this time of the year one could also add a couple of the flat white clusters of heavily scented elderflowers which are growing everywhere in the hedgerows, the scent is similar. Let the milk simmer for a few minutes then strain it into a clean pan.

Beat up the 4 egg yolks with 2 tablespoons of sugar, bring the milk almost to the boil and stir a little into the beaten egg yolks. Off the heat stir them into the milk and heat, stirring all the time, but without *quite* letting it boil, until it becomes thick enough to coat the back of a spoon. Don't let it boil as the eggs would scramble. Pour it into a pretty dish. When cold, spoon your floating islands as snowy whipped egg white on top. This is delicious. In winter when I have neither geranium nor elderflowers I usually simmer a strip of lemon peel in the milk.

The Week of the Salmon

Salmon is cheapest in July. "Cheap", is, of course, the wrong word for it as it is always expensive, but if you are going to have any at all, July is the best time. Two grilled salmon steaks with melted butter, cucumber salad and new potatoes would make a perfect little light supper to eat quietly with someone you love.

Avocado with Black Olives

I should begin the meal with a couple of avocado pears. Really I like mine to be quite plain – so ripe as to be almost squishy and just with a simple oil and lemon dressing, or perhaps some sauce hollandaise on them. I would not waste money on all those shrimps and things people put in them for I think it confuses the flavour. If you insist, however, on some sort of filling, try black olives in soured cream.

Using a stainless steel knife, cut the avocado lengthways through to the stone then separate the two halves by twisting them carefully in opposite directions. Take out the stone. Sprinkle the cut halves of the avocado, or avocados, with lemon juice so it does not discolour.

Stone and chop 100 g (4 oz) of black olives roughly – for two avocados. Stir them into a small carton of soured cream adding salt and pepper. Fill the avocados.

Grilled Salmon

You will need two 1·5 cm ($\frac{3}{4}$-inch) salmon steaks. Wipe them with a damp cloth. Sprinkle them with a little salt and pepper and chopped parsley. Line the grill pan with kitchen foil, brush this thickly with melted butter. Sprinkle a little sherry and, if available, some chopped fresh tarragon over each salmon steak. Make the griller very hot. Grill the salmon steaks about 15 cm (6 inches) from the heat for 7–10 minutes, do not turn them but baste them from time to time by spooning a little more melted butter over them – held ready in a small pan. This fish is done when it shrinks a bit from the bone and the flesh is pale and firm to the touch. When done lift them out on to a hot dish, garnish them with watercress. Have cucumber salad, new potatoes and either melted butter or sauce hollandaise to pour over them.

And for afters? What else but strawberries and cream?

A Moselle wine would be perfect with this meal, served chilled in its long green slender bottle– perhaps a *Bernkasteler Kurfurstlay Riesling* 1973, but there are heaps of others. Don't try to pronounce it, just write it down and show it to the man in the shop!

Last year some friends on holiday in Co. Cork went round to O'Flaherty's Bar, or the back of the Post Office, or wherever it might be that the Irish were quietly selling whole salmon – and it was on the last day so they bought a whole 5 kilo (14 lb) salmon very cheaply. They put it in an insulated picnic thing, brought it home and stuck it in the freezer. And I ate some of it with them at Christmas, hot with lots of melted butter and a very good parsley sauce. Of course frozen salmon is not so good as fresh, but it is still more fun and more original than turkey in December. They said it brought back all their holiday memories.

A Whole Salmon or Sea Trout in Foil

I usually cook a big piece of salmon or a whole salmon trout in foil in the oven. Salmon trout as the fish shops call it, or sea trout as most fly fishermen call it, is a slightly smaller, slightly cheaper fish. It too has pink flesh and, the experts say, a finer flavour.

Brush the fish over with melted butter, add salt and pepper, a squeeze of lemon juice, if liked, a small sliver – very small – of onion and a couple of sprigs of parsley and wrap it up completely in thickly buttered foil like a parcel.

Bake it in a moderate oven (180°C, 350°F, Mark 4). The exact time depends on the thickness rather than on the total weight of the fish. Allow about 40 minutes for a long slim salmon trout, about an hour for a thick piece of middle cut salmon – I am sorry not to be more exact. Towards the end open your foil parcel, and, very gently so as not to break the skin or the flesh, look inside it along the back bone, if the flesh is at all dark there, it is not cooked through, put it back in the oven for about another 15 minutes.

New Potatoes Baked in Butter

It is superb when served hot with new potatoes cooked in butter. Scrape the skin from about two dozen small new potatoes, rinse and pat them dry in a tea towel. Melt 100 g (4 oz) of butter in a heavy fireproof dish, add the potatoes with a little salt and pepper, rolling them in the liquid butter. Cover them with two thicknesses of foil pinching down the edges to seal them completely and then put a lid on top. Cook them in a moderate oven (180°C, 350°F, Mark 4) for 30–40 minutes, depending on the size of the potatoes. They are done when a fork goes in easily. Serve them hot and buttery sprinkled with chopped parsley.

Hollandaise Sauce

Hollandaise sauce is a classic with salmon or salmon trout and equally good in avocado pears or with hot, boiled, globe artichokes.

It is not half so difficult as you may have been led to believe.

Take a little pan with the yolk of an egg, the strained juice of a lemon, 1 dessertspoon of cold water, 3 dessertspoons of butter, some salt and pepper. Stand the pan in another containing very hot, but not boiling water. Beat the contents of the small pan with an egg whisk till the butter is melted. Then little by little, whipping all the time, add 5 dessertspoons of butter, cut in bits. The sauce should thicken like mayonnaise, but do whip right down to the bottom of the pan, and take care the water in the big pan doesn't bubble up into the little one.

Simple isn't it? Don't know what all the fuss is about. The sauce by the way is served *warm*, not hot, so if it has to wait don't try to heat it, just stand the little pan in another containing warm water, so it won't get cold. I always use a plain, wire, balloon-shaped egg whisk because I think the kind with a little wheel where you turn a handle doesn't get into the corners.

A Cold Collation

It's the sort of day when nothing moves except for a faint rustling of small leaves at the very top of the tree, and you can hear only the distant cooing of a party of pigeons over opposite in the beech thicket. A casual observer might think one was asleep. Not a bit of it. When I open my eyes I can see the fat, unwelcome form of Blue-bottle – or is it by now Son of Bluebottle – out for what he can get. Not much I can tell you. Any minute now I shall rouse myself enough to swat him with that Portuguese fly whisk we once bought in the back streets of Lisbon. Then I shall go in and cook something totally effortless and absolutely fabulous for lunch.

A Cold Collation perhaps. This will just be diced chicken mixed with some chilled green grapes and shelled walnuts then turned in a dressing of whipped cream mixed with salt, pepper and a little lemon juice. It will be served in large, chilled wine glasses. Lovely!

Chilled Green Pea Soup

Or perhaps, if I could rouse myself sufficiently to peel and chop a very small onion, we shall have chilled green pea soup. For this chop your little onion and let it simmer in 500 ml (1 pint) of stock with 200 g (8 oz) of frozen peas for about 5 minutes with salt, pepper and celery salt to your taste. Then you just purée the soup in the electric mixer and chill it. When it is really cold stir in 4 tablespoons of thick cream. Easy isn't it. One can almost eat it in one's sleep.

The heat and stillness of a long, dry summer gives one an inescapable feeling of evanescence. These, you say to yourself, are the longest days; in a few weeks the nights will be drawing in. Already the irises are over and the long grass is cut almost before the strawberries are ripe. It cannot last. Very probably these *are* the Good Old Days for one has this sense of calm, of stillness, as though in the centre of some trough, or peak maybe, of atmospheric pressure. It is as if one were waiting for thunder and lightning or some sort of mid-summer storm. And yet it doesn't rain.

Devonshire Junket

A plain, cool, Devonshire junket, now deeply out of fashion and considered "down market" in some parts of the country, is one of my standbys in sweltering summer. It is absolutely no trouble, and makes a cool and delicate dish which looks quite elegant in one of those fluted, white china, soufflé dishes. It used to be known in Scotland as Cold Velvet Cream. You simply buy a bottle of rennet essence from the grocer, it's quite cheap and keeps for months after it has been opened, though not for ever of course. Mix a tablespoon of rum with 1 litre (2 pints) of fresh milk at blood heat, add a tablespoon of sugar and 2 teaspoons of rennet. Stir it and then just leave it to stand at room temperature, not in the fridge. That's all!

Instead of rum it may be flavoured with the grated rind of a lemon or simply with 2 fresh bay leaves and a good pinch of grated nutmeg. This spreads over the top and they look very pretty together. The milk, however, must not boil, nor have been boiled, or it will not set, and should you wish to test the temperature I must say the simplest way is to dip a clean finger in it. If the milk feels neither hot nor cold then it's at blood heat. "'Tis an ill cook who cannot lick his own fingers," as William Shakespeare said.

When the junket has set you could spread whipped or clotted

cream carefully over the top, sprinkle it with grated nutmeg and caster sugar and garnish it with brandy snaps or ratafia biscuits, but this is for very grand occasions.

Lemon Solid

Lemon Solid is another of these old-fashioned country set creams which used to be popular in English villages for tea with some of the soft fruit. Warm 500 ml (1 pint) of milk, stirring in the grated rind of 2 lemons, 12 g (½-oz) of gelatine and 150 g (6 oz) of sugar. Heat it gently, stirring, until both gelatine and sugar have melted properly. Now add the strained juice of the two lemons and stir for a moment until the curd separates. Pour it into a bowl and turn it out when set. I suppose from the simplicity and cheapness of the recipe, that you cannot possibly guess how good it is.

Honeycomb Mould

It is like the old-fashioned Honeycomb Mould that we used to have in my childhood with hot stewed raspberries. You put these in the warm oven with sugar, but no liquid, and just leave them till the juice runs out. Cream is almost superfluous with them.

The old Honeycomb Mould of long forgotten summers is equally delicious though it does take a little longer to make. Heat up 500 ml (1 pint) of milk with the grated rind of a lemon and, if you like, a bay leaf from the garden. Sprinkle 4 teaspoons of gelatine into 4 tablespoons of boiling water, stir till it melts. Beat up 3 egg yolks with 75 g (3 oz) of caster sugar, put them in the top of a double saucepan with hot, but not quite boiling, water in the pan beneath. Stir in the warm milk and cook, stirring all the time, until it thickens enough to coat the back of a spoon. Take it off the heat and for heaven's sake don't let it boil as it would curdle at once and go lumpy like a sort of scrambled egg. If you have no double saucepan, use a basin standing in a bowl of simmering water. Add the melted gelatine then gently mix or fold in the three egg whites whipped so stiff the basin may be turned upside down without them falling out. Pour it into a 1 litre (2 pint) mould or basin rinsed with water, leave it in a cool place or in the refrigerator to set before turning it out.

This pretty pudding separates into two parts, one frothy and the other lemony and is delicious whether or not eaten with fruit from the back garden. You could make it now and then go back to sleep under a tree while the pudding sets.

Mykonos

We danced in the streets of Mykonos. It is one of the Isles of Greece. Stark white, burnt brown, very hot and full of hippies. I think they sleep on the beach. The houses and parts of the street which have been painted white (for tourists) almost knock your eye out at mid-day – dazzling, blinding, glaring white, and full of boutiques with hand-woven smocks and gilt jewellery copied from the antique. And un-like most Greek islands it is free of wasps.

We were with a Greek university professor from California, full of nostalgia for the place where he was born. "My father was a sea captain," he said, becoming more and more Greek as he spoke. "We have this great love of the sea, we Greeks, *Thalassia*, since Ulysses, since classic times . . ."

It was an absolutely gorgeous meal which we ate in three – or was it four? – different restaurants, and which I shall remember all my life. Earlier we had been in a small, sweltering bus to the beach several miles from the harbour, past unbelievably dusty, baked earth, divided into small, dried-up fields with spiky windmills, motionless in the heat.

In the beach café, out of the hot sun, we had sat under a vine or something, drinking ouzo, and nibbling black olives and grilled squid off a platter. It was far too hot for lunch. The Greeks have ouzo neat, with water as a chaser, and bring you little glasses of iced water (like with the coffee in Vienna). Not being Greek, I poured the water into mine and asked for an ice cube too. Then the ouzo goes cloudy like the pastis you get in the South of France, and it tastes of aniseed too.

In the evening there was a faint breeze, and we wandered from one restaurant to another looking at the fresh fish and the cooked dishes in the refrigerator cabinets and tasting the *Mezes*, which they bring you with a bottle of wine. Stuffed vine leaves, sliced tomatoes, tiny meat balls with toothpicks, pieces of delicately seasoned octopus and tiny stuffed marrows no bigger than a thumb. With it they bring you a delicate, cold, creamy sauce called *Tahini*, made from sesame seeds, like a cross between mayonnaise and peanut butter. In this we dipped pieces of bread and fingers of raw carrot. It is absolutely delicious and you can get it in jars quite cheaply from Greek provision shops in England.

There are men who stand at the street corners with little charcoal stoves cooking *souvlakia* – chunks of lamb, pork, chicken or swordfish threaded on skewers between bay leaves and rolled in oil before cooking.

Later we clasped hands and did a lovely Greek dance, the name of which I have forgotten, to the sound of the Bazouki music floating out of the cafés.

Then in a side street we found a place with a lobster to our liking (or rather a crawfish, one of those things with waving feelers). We paid a deposit and went off to have a drink promising to come back when it was cooked. It was an expensive meal to celebrate our American friend's return to Greece, and because he had bought a Greek sailor's hat (with peak), wearing it proudly during dinner. "After all," he said, "we are sitting in the street."

Apart from the hot-boiled lobster, there was a country salad – chunks of tomato, sliced onion, pieces of paprika pepper, black olives and hard-boiled eggs, tossed in a mixture of oil and lemon juice with salt and pepper. There was a bowl of chilled yoghourt mixed with salt and pepper and chopped mint with lots of grated cucumber in it.

There was a plate of fetta cheese, very salty and chalk white, for crumbling over the salad, and there was a bowl of *skorthalia* or garlic sauce, which is delicious on grilled or spit-roasted chicken as well as lobster, or crab, or with cold meat. They dip their bread in the wine, the Greeks, or in oil and lemon, and sometimes rub it with a bit of garlic, munching it with the cheese, the wine, and a few grapes.

It was a marvellous evening with two bottles of chilled golden Retsina wine. This is heavily flavoured with resin and is very like the smell of pine trees and warm pine needles in the sun. In the old days when Greek wine was still stored in goat skins, they poured resin on top to caulk them. This flavoured the wine. Now it is kept in oak casks they still add the resin for flavour. You can buy Retsina from wine merchants in England, and it is a drink I like occasionally. The Greeks usually add water to it in the hot summer months, as they have done since classic times. Neat wine in hot weather, they say, is unhealthy.

As we sat there people came round selling fresh fish – sea urchins, clams and one thing or another. Later, we sat down on the quay at café tables eating sweet pastries, drinking black coffee, and gazing at the now wine-dark sea. It was very late.

You could do a whole Greek meal on a barbecue in the garden. Or part of it on the barbecue and part of it under the griller in the kitchen. Have slices of fresh melon, peaches and other fruit. Turkish coffee, white wine and soda water.

Greek Sauce for Country Salad

Olive oil, strained lemon juice, salt and pepper, shaken up in a screw-top bottle until it goes sort of creamy. Dead simple. Excellent, too, poured on crisp dry grilled fish, done on the barbecue.

Souvlakia

Cut up about 200 g (8 oz) of chicken or pork fillet or both in chunks as big as a walnut, roll them in olive oil, salt and pepper, and chopped mint, leave them at least half an hour, thread them on skewers sandwiched with bay leaves, chunks of onion and tomato. Then grill them over a fierce heat on a charcoal barbecue or in the kitchen grill, keep turning them so the meat cooks evenly and is almost charred outside but still juicy in the middle. Eat them the minute they are done otherwise the meat gets tough and chewy.

Skorthalia or Garlic Sauce

For grilled chicken, grilled squid, grilled chops or souvlakia made with lamb. Beat 6 peeled garlic cloves and a teaspoon of salt to a paste and add two tablespoons of soft white breadcrumbs, and gradually pour in ¾-cup of olive oil and the juice of a lemon alternately, beating as you go with a wooden spoon, as if you were making mayonnaise. Add salt and pepper.

Greek Coffee

Tiny cups of strong black coffee are the popular drink all over Greece. It is made and served from a brass pot or *briki* which tapers at the top to let the coffee boil quickly and throw up a heavy froth. They serve it in very, very small black coffee cups, pouring a little at a time into each cup so the froth is equally divided. Usually glasses of ice-cold water are served with it because, in fact, sweet coffee makes you thirsty.

Ask for *Métrios* if you want your Greek coffee medium strong with only a "little" sugar; *Séktos* without sugar; *Varis Glykus* extremely sweet.

Warm the coffee pot. Use the tiny coffee cups for measuring. Add only as many cups of water as there will be cups of coffee. Add 1 teaspoon sugar per cup and let it boil. Then add a good heaped teaspoon of the special powder ground coffee per cup of water. Let it boil and froth up to the top of the pot and serve at once. It does not need straining as the coffee is so fine. The blend is not so important as the way it is ground – pulverized to dust in a special machine. Good grocers and delicatessen shops in Britain will usually grind it like this for you on request.

Avgolemono

There are always lemons and black olives on the table in Greece. You sprinkle lemon juice on the superb, creamy goat's milk yoghourt, as thick as junket, that they serve on request for breakfast. You squeeze them over kebabs. And you use them to thicken *Avgolemono* – a delicious but simple lemon soup made with chicken. You need some good chicken broth. I serve the chicken afterwards covered in homemade mayonnaise, for which I use lemon not vinegar. A chicken bouillon cube would do for this soup, but it will not be quite so good.

Heat the stock together with a handful of rice and let it simmer for about 10 minutes till the rice is cooked. Then, just before serving, beat up the yolks of two eggs with the strained juice of 1½ lemons. Stir in a little of the warm stock and then gradually add the mixture, stirring, to your pan of chicken broth. Heat, stirring, for a few moments. Serve it if you like with fried bread croutons.

My Old Friend Mrs X

My old friend Mrs X is about 80 with a round, smiling face like a red apple and she still has one of those old kitchen stoves you have to do with black lead. Serious cooking is done on a modern gas stove half its size, but she still does the hearth startlingly white with donkey stone and used, until recently, to make a kind of lace pattern with it round the place where her cat usually eats. "Got too old to be up to them larks now," she told me, "like gardening, never could be bothered with that. No time. I am too interested in my inner man!"

And indeed one of her main interests is, and always has been, cooking, so that sometimes when I get a broad daylight view of her – large, well-nourished and one of the few women I have ever known who is able to wear one of those loose tent coats as a fitted jacket – I get a little worried whether I had better take to gardening before it is too late.

"Been making scruggin cake," my old friend went on this week rather breathlessly. She's always breathless, it's the weight. "Make all my own. Got jars and jars of pickles too. Never eat them myself though. Keep them to give to people who do things for me."

Scruggins (of course) are a country speciality from the Welsh border, the crisp little pieces of fat or crackling left after pig's flair fat has been melted down for lard and dripping, what in the Midlands are called pork scratchings. They are not only very good to eat but very cheap. When made crisp in the oven and rolled in salt they go with an aperitif and should be rescued from obscurity.

Scruggins Cake

For scruggins cake put 400 g (1 lb) of self-raising flour in the mixing bowl with 200 g (8 oz) of granulated sugar and 300 g (12 oz) of scruggins, or scratchings, chopped up in small pieces. Stir and make it into a soft dough with milk and water then roll it out about 2·5 cm (1 inch) thick and press it into a square tin well greased with lard. Sprinkle the top of your cake with a little caster sugar, and mark it into squares. Bake it for 30 minutes in a moderate oven (180°C, 350°F, Mark 4).

Cider Cake

Mrs X's old-fashioned cider cake should be made with rough draught cider or "scrumpy" when it has an equally distinctive flavour. Bottle cider can be used if fairly dry, but is not so tasty in the cake.

You must first cream 100 g (4 oz) of sugar and 100 g (4 oz) of butter and then add two well beaten eggs. Sift 200 g (8 oz) flour with 1 teaspoon of bicarbonate of soda and half nutmeg grated and add half of this to the other mixture, then beat up a teacup of cider to a froth and add that before sifting in the other 100 g (4 oz) of flour. Mix it well, bake it in a shallow well-greased tin for 45 minutes in a moderate oven (180°C, 350°F, Mark 4).

Pickled Walnuts

If you can get any fresh green walnuts I suggest you pickle them as my old friend does. The finished result, she says, is worth its weight in gold locally. You want green walnuts which are still soft right through and you should be able to run a darning needle through them easily when the barrow boy is not looking. And let me say here and now there's no need to prick them all over with a pin. Buy some block salt if you can get it and make a brine solution with 150 g (6 oz) of salt to 1 litre (2 pints) of water. Leave the walnuts in it for nine days. Change the brine twice and stir it up night and morning.

Then drain them into a colander and rinse them by pouring hot water over them. Stand them in the sun or air on trays till they go black. Put a tablespoonful of mixed pickling spice and 2 chopped nutmegs in a muslin bag. Boil this in an enamel or stainless steel pan in enough vinegar to cover them. You will need about 1 litre (2 pints) for 50 walnuts. Pack them into warm jars and strain the hot vinegar over them. Screw down the tops when cold and put a bit of paper between them and the vinegar.

Autumn

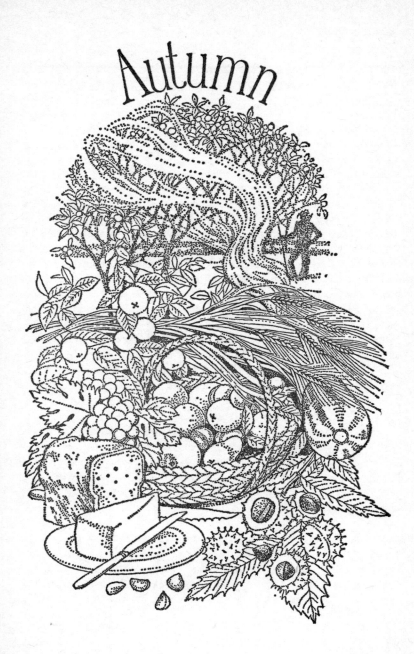

Shopping on Sunday Morning

It would be great fun if we had street markets on Sunday mornings in English country towns. It is the most delightful way imaginable of buying the Sunday lunch and you can fit your purchases to the appetite of the moment. In Caen, Normandy, as in many other French provincial towns, there are on Sunday mornings stalls piled high with everything from black puddings to plastic hosepipe. All the food shops are open and bulging with pots of *tripes à la mode de Caen* that you can buy and re-heat at home in the oven. There is potted pork, chocolate cakes, and babas soaked in rum. Delicious little legs of lamb from the salt marshes and sweet shops full of those pretty white boxes of almond fondants, some arranged with a cross shape of foil in the middle, which the French buy for christenings.

In France the shops which open on Sunday mornings close all day Monday. There are people with baskets of sparkling fresh, practically flapping, fish. You can get pot plants and cut flowers, pigs' trotters rolled in breadcrumbs, flat oval dishes with a mound of duck pâté in the middle and the sides all glistening with luscious meat jelly. It is absolutely delicious.

Afterwards you can go into one of the little restaurants with the red checked gingham curtains and feast on the local delicacies. *Sole Normande*, for instance, a dish endlessly elaborated by great chefs in Paris, but best I think when simply cooked as they do it on the spot.

Sole Normande

Just poach the fillets of sole in a fireproof dish in the oven. Four medium fillets will need about half a glass of slightly salted water and take 8–10 minutes in a pre-heated moderate oven (180°C, 350°F, Mark 4). They should have a bit of paper, or the backbones, laid on top to keep them moist. In Normandy they often add a handful of raw, well-scrubbed mussels as well. When cooked, drain the fish well, shell the now open mussels. Put both back in the oven for a moment to dry, then add a classic *Sauce Normande* just before serving.

Sauce Normande

Put 125 g (5 oz) of butter cut in pieces in a little pan with 125 ml
(¼-pint) of thick cream, salt and pepper and 2 raw egg yolks. Let it all
melt over a low heat stirring all the time and cooking it very carefully for about 4 minutes. Do not let it get too hot or you will just
have rich scrambled eggs.

The dish is at its very best when prepared with what we call Dover
sole, but the same recipe can be used for a piece of skate or turbot or
cod cutlets, whiting or even a bit of plaice would do. They use the
same rich sauce on French beans and Jerusalem artichokes, or
plainly boiled white turnips cut in chunks. Any of these would go
perfectly with lamb chops or roast stuffed rabbit. Boil the French
beans in salted water and drain them before stirring them into the
sauce. Scarlet runners should be strung and broken into 2–3 cm
(1 inch) lengths, not sliced, before cooking.

Normandy is the part of France I love most. It is not only the
gorgeous cooking but the friendly people, and the slate-roofed,
white-shuttered farmhouses made from the same grey Caen stone as
many English cathedrals. When he died in 1087, William the
Conqueror himself was buried in St Steven's Cathedral in Caen, and
you can see his tomb in front of the altar. Everybody swears that
there are one or two of his bones in it. During the Liberation the
people of Caen took refuge in the vaults there, following the parish
priest, and kept their lives, faith and hope in the crypt under William
the Conqueror. You see, no one believed the English would shell it,
for legend says if St Steven's falls the British monarchy will collapse.

It is a rich farming country squelching with cream and butter
which they use for all their cooking. They pour Calvados or apple
brandy in the middle of a baked apple dumpling then eat it with
cream. There are omelettes flamed in Calvados and served with
buttered apples, smoked chitterling sausages – the famous *andouilles
de Vire* – served sliced for starters with a plate of shrimps, hunks of
bread and the bland local butter from Isigny.

Coquelet Normande

Cut a small roasting chicken in portions. Brown these gently in

100 g (4 oz) of frothy butter in a fireproof dish. Sprinkle it with salt and pepper. When just golden put a lid on. Cook it gently in the butter for about 30 minutes, then flame it by pouring 2 tablespoons of warmed Calvados over it and setting light to this. Brandy or whisky could be used, though the taste will be a bit different. Add 250 ml (½-pint) of single cream, heating, stirring and scraping the pan with a wooden spoon to get all the glorious gubbins off the bottom. Taste for seasoning and pour it over the chicken.

Some cooks also add 6 or 7 whole button onions and 200 g (8 oz) of whole button mushrooms, cooked separately in butter. And there is a version from the *Vallée d'Auge* which contains buttered apples.

But the food everywhere is marvellous. Last time I visited the Lion d'Or in Bayeux, I saw the legs of one of the tables in the dining-room break under the weight of the food! They serve crisp *pommes sablées* with their chicken in cream and mushrooms.

Pommes Sablées

Half-boil some large, peeled, or scraped, potatoes. Put them in a shallow fireproof dish with a little chicken stock. Could be a bouillon cube. Add nuts of butter and grate a little heap of cheese on top of each potato. Put them in a hot oven, basting with the buttery stock until mostly evaporated. In France a plain tossed salad would be served with these rather than a second vegetable.

Calvados

Calvados, which is distilled from apples, is drunk in the middle of these vast meals in Normandy to settle the digestion and revive the appetite.

At one time all the farms used to make it and I once bought a bottle in a garage near Fécamp which had been distilled by the man's aunty, and practically took the varnish off the dinner-table. The good ones, however, are aged in barrels and some of the 10- to 15-year-old ones are marvellous. A good Calvados must be reddish and not smell earthy, you rub it on the back of your hand to heat it and get the bouquet (almost as if you were choosing scent), before swallowing it neat.

When I suggested in Normandy that one might try it with a little soda they looked at me as if I were mad. "Calvados," my friend Monsieur Toutain said, "is a life's study. I think it is better than Cognac. I found a marvellous barrel of very old Calvados in a cellar during the Liberation," he went on, taking off his glasses and polishing them wistfully at the very thought of it. "It is sometimes made on farms even today, though, of course, mostly at the distilleries. Traditionally, in Normandy, if you have five apple trees, you have the right to make your own Calvados, but it is a right which now dies out with the farmer, his son does not inherit it. And it is hardly drunk by the young people any more."

And what do you have for afters? Well, a bit of cheese. Perhaps a slice of soft rich *Livarot* or *Pont l'Eveque* or the slightly milder *Camembert* or a piece of *Fromage de Monsieur*, or *St Paulin*, all of which are made locally. Add some crusty French bread and a raw apple to munch with it.

Much Ado About Marrows

Marrows are quite cheap in Autumn and when not too big can taste as good as those little courgettes or baby marrows one gets in fashionable restaurants. Marrows, like pumpkins, can be stored as they are on a shelf in a cool shed or larder for some months. Do not, however, cook them in water, the vegetable is watery enough.

Buttered Marrow

Chop it up, if it is young and tender you probably need not peel it but you should get rid of the pips. Put it in a pan with salt, pepper, a chopped onion, some knobs of butter and a little chopped parsley. Let it simmer very gently with a lid on. Stir occasionally. No liquid is necessary, enough comes out of the marrow to stop it from burning if done on a low heat.

Marrow and Cheese

A big marrow can be done very nicely with cheese. Peel and slice it into a casserole that has been rubbed round with cut onion or a piece of garlic. Then over the layer of marrow put a thick layer of grated cheese, then more marrow and more cheese till the dish is full. Finish it with grated cheese and a few breadcrumbs. Dot it liberally with butter and bake it in a moderate oven (180°C, 350°F, Mark 4) until the marrow is soft and the cheese has melted into it in 35–40 minutes. A perfectly delicious dish.

Italian Marrow

It is very good too, done in the Italian way with tomatoes, oil and garlic. Chop it in chunks, peeling it if necessary and getting rid of the seeds. Frizzle some chopped garlic in a couple of tablespoons of cooking oil. Add the marrow with 3 or 4 sliced tomatoes (or a table-spoon of tomato purée mixed with half a cup of water). Sprinkle the top thickly with grated cheese and bake it in a moderate oven (180°C, 350°F, Mark 4) for 35–40 minutes. It makes a very good light supper dish and would be excellent with a tossed salad served on side plates.

Canal Fare

It is a wide open landscape, with larks rising and hump-backed bridges over the Grand Union Canal. At Leighton Buzzard I found a man who still paints those brightly-coloured roses and castles on the narrow boats. There are still a few left carrying coal to the paper mills and a jam factory in London from the village of Croxley near Coventry. The whole round trip takes about a week; several boats passed while I was there, linked in loaded pairs with long-haired men at the tiller and sometimes with a lean shaggy dog following them along the tow path. There are no horses now, they use Diesel engines, but the boats' three cornered cratches which hold up the long planks and sheeting are still brilliantly painted with roses and lozenges. Some of the butty cabins still have clusters of lace-edged plates hung thick around the walls, and are all decorated with fairytale castles.

Joe Harrison who works for the Wyvern Shipping Co., a small firm on the canal bank, does them with a free hand and uses ordinary gutsy, marine paints in the traditional manner. I bought one of his painted buckets for my own kitchen. It's grass green with a scarlet base and handle and there are big splodgy blue, yellow and red roses done thick all over it. But there are not many working boats left now and when I got there he had just finished doing the two back panels of somebody's Mini Estate Van with two large bunches of yellow roses.

The great gastronomical favourite of the old narrow boatmen was the "Pail Dinner". It was very practical if space was limited for the entire dinner could be cooked in one dinner pail, which also supplied the washing-up water.

Pail Dinners

The cook used to stand a can or an old jam jar in the bottom of the pail, filling it first with a layer of turnips and cut rabbit or bacon hock, then fingers of carrots and parsnip. She filled it and the bucket with water and brought it all gently to the boil while she made a lid of suet pastry which was laid across the simmering meat and veg. By the time the pastry had risen the peeled potatoes could be put on top, then more pastry. The potatoes were steamed between two layers of it. On top finally she put some peeled apples, tied a cloth on top and left it for about 2 hours to cook. It was delicious. Hot broth. Then meat and vegetables in suet pastry and finally a hot apple pudding all ready at once.

Pot pies done in a heavy iron saucepan were another old favourite on the inland waterways. They are a sort of mixed stew of meat and vegetables with a round flat piece of suet pastry laid across the top when the stew is almost cooked. And narrow-boat wives used to be dab hands at the old bag puddings too. These are boiled suet puddings, perhaps with beefsteak and mushrooms, made in a floured cloth not a basin. The cloth was hung from a wooden spoon in boiling water or a broth to cook.

I lunched at a local inn and spent some time afterwards enjoying the Autumn sunshine outside Leighton Buzzard Parish Church. It is one of those empty country churchyards full of grass and silence. The roof inside is thick with carved and painted angels all with wooden wings, some furled, others ready to take off like a flight of pigeons. The vicar said that there had never been any buzzards there and that they had nothing to do with the place.

Nowadays Leighton Buzzard has no poultry market either, although there are stall holders all down the main street on Tuesdays selling everything from sunflower seeds to broken biscuits. I bought a lot of pink Victoria and purple plums and made some of them into fritters.

Plum Fritters

You have to cut the big plums in half and take out the stones after peeling them. Both peaches and plums are easy to peel if you plunge them in boiling water for a few seconds; the skin then comes off easily with a pointed knife. Dip them in thickish pancake batter and fry them in hot oil or lard. Drain them on kitchen paper or a tea towel and serve them at once rolled in grated chocolate and caster sugar. Peaches also make lovely fritters done in the same way. Apples or pears should be peeled, cored and cut in rings then dipped in batter and fried. They need no grated chocolate, just a little sugar, though I, being a north country woman, like to eat a bit of crumbly red Cheshire or Wensleydale cheese with my apple fritters.

Apple Rings

Apple rings, with the fruit peeled and cored and cut in rounds as for fritters, are very good with Black Puddings or pork chops. You just dip them in egg, then breadcrumbs and fry them as before.

Not What You Think

It must have been the very first thing that I learned to cook. Years and years ago at school in Switzerland, and I can still remember the cosy smell of hot pastry, of warm apples, and grated lemon peel as they mingled with the rich appetizing odours of whatever else we were going to have for lunch. The traditional French *tarte aux pommes*. You still find it almost everywhere in Paris in lovely, old-fashioned restaurants like Vagenende, in the Boulevard Saint Germain, in little cafés round the Boulevard Saint Michel, and in almost every bistro, to complete the inevitable meal of *potage aux legumes*, pork chops and a vast selection of cheese.

Even though, one must report sadly, big ice-cream factories have been so successful in Paris that now every restaurant has Italian cassata and about half a dozen others on the menu. The ices are quite good, but the old desserts are being pushed out, and·manufactured food is making disastrous inroads on French cooking, as it is everywhere else.

But a big French *tarte aux pommes*, brown and glistening with apricot jam spread warm and thick over the top, looks most appetizing as it lies on the centre table of a restaurant beside the bottles of cognac and the potted plants. And it is better than spending a lot of money on the flowers, which are not edible. It is quite easy if perhaps a bit tedious to make, though I always enjoy doing it. Recipes vary in different parts of France, but this is the most popular.

Tarte aux Pommes

Mix shortcrust pastry in the proportions of 200 g (8 oz) plain flour to 100 g (4 oz) butter. It is best mixed with a beaten egg instead of water, and one can add a tablespoon of sugar.

For a big rectangular tart, butter the inside of a long swiss-roll tin, line it with shortcrust pastry, pricking the pastry base with a fork. Peel, core and quarter about 800 g (2 lb) of eating apples, dropping them in a bowl of cold water as you go. Then slice them into thin half-moons, and lay them in neat, overlapping rows like slates on a roof down the length of the tin. Turn it round and do the same again so the next row faces in the opposite direction. Repeat until the tin is full.

Put the tart in the oven as soon as it is garnished, or the juice oozing out of the apples will make the pastry wet. Bake it for about 30 minutes in a pre-heated, fairly hot oven (190°C, 375°F, Mark 5). After cooking, sprinkle the tart with sugar or a little apricot jelly simmered with sugar and the peel and cores of the apples, till you have a thin yellow syrup. If you cannot get the apricot jelly, use thin, clear marmalade, without the peel.

For a round *tarte aux pommes* you need a greased metal baking sheet and a greased flan ring. This is a circle of metal about 2·5 cm (1 inch) deep and 15–25 cm (6–10 inches) across, depending on how big a tart you want. Lay it on the baking sheet, put the pastry and the apples in the middle (laying the apple slices in rings, starting from the outside and working in towards the centre). Then, when cooked, you can slide the tart off easily with a fish slice.

When you make French apple tart in a solid tin it is difficult to get it out in one piece. Those fluted earthenware dishes they sell for it in expensive pottery shops, though pretty, are hopeless. Madame de Saint-Ange warned French cooks about these in a famous book about 40 years ago. If you cannot buy a flan ring, get a strip of kitchen foil, fold it in several thicknesses to make a 2–3 cm (1 inch) deep strip and bend this round into a circle.

The gorgeous tart you get in Strasbourg or at the famous Brasserie Flo, in Paris, is made with very sweet shortcrust pastry and has a rich cream filling.

Tarte à l'Alsacienne

Garnish the tart with apples as before, bake it in a pre-heated hot oven (200°C, 400°F, Mark 6) for 15 minutes. Meanwhile beat up 125 ml (¼-pint) of thick cream with 1 tablespoon sugar, 2 egg yolks, and either a pinch of cinnamon and some grated lemon rind, or 1 tablespoon of Kirsch liqueur. After the preliminary baking pour this over the apples, finish cooking it in a moderate oven (180°C, 350°F, Mark 4) until the cream is set and slightly golden.

The best of these tarts are not only flavoured with Kirsch but have warm Kirsch poured over them just before serving. They are then set alight so they come flaming to the table. Kirsch is a clear, dry, white spirit distilled from wild cherries. The stones, which are crushed with the fruit, give it an almost almond flavour. Unfortunately, though you can get excellent cooking Kirsch in Continental grocers' shops, it is expensive in this country, so one must use something else instead.

The *tarte des Demoiselles Tatin* is a kind of upside down apple pie – a country thing from Central France near the cathedral town of Bourges. I don't think anyone remembers who the Demoiselles actually were but this is how you make it.

Tarte des Demoiselles Tatin

Make your pastry from 200 g (8 oz) flour, 40 g (1½ oz) caster sugar, 150 g (6 oz) butter, a dessertspoon of cooking oil and a little hot water to mix. Chill for several hours before rolling it out. The tart starts off on top of the stove but is finished in the oven. You need a heavy, round, shallow fireproof dish for it. Peel, core and quarter 1 kilo (2½ lb) of *eating* apples. Put 125 g (5 oz) of butter and 125 g (5 oz) of sugar in the fireproof dish. Pack the apples tightly in it, simmer over a low heat (with an asbestos mat). They smell heavenly sizzling in the hot butter. The caramelized sugar gradually rises to the top. Do not stir them. Now cover them with your pastry. Bake the tart in a hot oven (200°C, 400°F, Mark 6) for 10–15 minutes. Take it out and reverse it on to a nice plate. It is at its best served just warm. The apples go all dark and are quite delicious.

Cooking with Saffron

I remember seeing thousands and thousands of them once in a field in the North of Spain on the edge of the sea. I suppose they had been growing there for hundreds of years, for they were so tightly packed you could not have crossed the field without stepping on them – the autumn, or saffron, crocus that nurserymen are trying to get us to plant. It was near Cap Finisterre and as the breeze blew in from the Atlantic you got a strong but pleasant, bitter-sweet smell from them.

As one travels south in Autumn, along the route to Spain and down through France, past houses crimson with Virginia creeper and hung with paprika peppers and smaller scarlet chilli peppers drying in the sun, you see great rosy-lilac autumn crocuses fluttering thickly by the wayside. There are a lot of them all over France, in Flanders and, thick in the fields, around Sedan. I think some of them are not real autumn crocuses at all, but the wickedly beautiful *colchicum*, a sort of autumn lily which poisons cattle and is now used pharmaceutically for doubling the chromosomes in plants.

They use saffron a lot in Spanish cooking. It was introduced into Spain by the Arabs, and it has an unmistakable, slightly bitter taste. It appears in most of those garlicky fish soups we get in Spain and

Italy and the South of France, and is indispensable for *paella* and *risotto alla Milanese*. It was once used for colouring cheese and butter and the ancient Greeks used it to dye cloth. Spanish grocers sell tiny, brightly printed packets hardly bigger than a postage stamp containing about a score of dried saffron thread or crocus stems. Three or four are enough to colour and flavour about 400 g (1 lb) of rice. As 60- to 80,000 flowers are needed to produce about 90 g (3½ oz) of dried saffron and they are all gathered by hand, it is the most expensive of all spices, so it is fortunate that you do not need much of it. A lot of saffron powder sold is a fake, so it is better to buy the little dried stamens or threads as you cannot imitate these.

The classic Italian *risotto alla Milanese* is always made with chicken broth and flavoured with saffron, which makes the rice bright yellow. Some risottos are heaped up with mussels, fried chicken livers, mushrooms, prawns and things, but when well made it is very good just plain with lots of melted butter and cheese.

Risotto alla Milanese

Put 2 tablespoons of butter in a large pan and in it "melt" a sliced onion until it is soft and golden. Pour in 75 g (3 oz) of Patna or Italian rice per person stirring until buttery and the grains coated. Then start adding hot chicken stock from a pan, a cupful at a time. You can make risotto with chicken bouillon cubes. But a tinned, whole chicken makes a better one, using the jellied stock, and chicken fat from the tin, then stirring in the chicken pieces taken from the bone – they fall off anyway. Watch the rice, adding more hot stock as it evaporates. 400 g (1 lb) of rice absorbs about 1 l 250 ml (2½ pints) of liquid, taking 30–35 minutes to cook. Add a little hot water if the stock runs out or a cup of white wine if you wish; when the rice is soft add the saffron.

Soak four or five saffron stamens in a coffee cup of hot water, mash them, then stir into the rice. Now add 100 g (4 oz) each of butter and grated cheese. Hand around more grated cheese for people to sprinkle over it.

The Spaniards have a deliciously simple way of using saffron – Saffron Potatoes.

Saffron Potatoes

Take 4 large, hot, baked, jacket potatoes, cut off the tops, scoop out the insides, mix with salt, pepper, lots of butter, and two or three crushed saffron threads (or a pinch of powder), mixed with a tablespoon of hot water. Heap the mixture back into the skins leaving a hollow in the middle of each. Break an egg in each, put the potatoes into the oven until the eggs have just set. Serve piping hot in a folded napkin garnished with watercress.

A good paella is the great Spanish dish for feast days. Marvellous for a party, it is too expensive for people to eat there every day. Almost anything can go into it and it should be made for at least six people in a flat dish called a *paellera*, like a frying pan with no handle or a small dustbin lid, but any shallow fireproof dish will do.

Paella

Cut a chicken into about eight portions. Fry them gently in the shallow pan in 125 ml (¼-pint) of olive oil with a chopped onion, sliced paprika pepper (with the seeds removed), 2 diced bacon rashers. And, if you like, a sliced, cleaned cuttlefish. Well, it has a lovely flavour! Add 2 chopped garlic cloves, a handful of peas, or French beans cut in chunks, 2 sliced tomatoes, and 100 g (4 oz) of mushrooms, or some Spanish sausage, then when everything is cooking nicely, nearly 400 g (1 lb) of rice.

Arrange it all in your shallow dish. Add a good litre (2 pints) of boiling water or of chicken stock so the rice is well covered, then the four or five saffron stamens crushed and soaked in a coffee cup of hot water as before. Take care not to stir it once the boiling liquid has been added.

Arrange some of the following nicely on the rice: 100 g (4 oz) prawns, or scallops, or scampi, or crab pieces, or black olives. A litre (2 pints) of raw cockles or mussels, (well washed in plenty of running water with the whiskers cut off and any open or broken ones thrown away – the shells will open in cooking). Sprinkle the top with chopped parsley and put the whole thing in a moderate oven (180°C, 350°F, Mark 4) for about 40 minutes till the liquid has disappeared, the rice is cooked and bright yellow and almost toasty on top. You can drink masses of cheap Spanish wine with this.

Catherine of Aragon (who was, you remember, a Spanish princess) went to live in Bedfordshire after her divorce, and spent the years of boredom in teaching the villagers to make lace and grow saffron crocuses. The growers were called "crokers". This part of England was once famous for it and the town of Saffron Walden in nearby Essex took its name from the once flourishing local industry. I am not sure what we used saffron for in England in those days, but the Cornish Saffron Bread made at Easter is coloured with it. I wish people would make it more often.

Cornish Saffron Bread

Sift 450 g (1 lb 2 oz) of flour, a pinch of salt and nutmeg in a warm bowl. Work in 100 g (4 oz) of butter, 100 g (4 oz) lard as for pastry. Add 50 g (2 oz) peel, 150 g (6 oz) currants. Cream 12 g ($\frac{1}{2}$-oz) yeast with 75 g (3 oz) sugar; when liquid, add a little tepid milk. Pour this in a hole in the centre of the flour mixture. Mix with your hands to a sticky dough. Add the saffron in warm water as before. Beat and slap the dough with your hands. Knead for five minutes on a floured board.

Leave it for 1 hour in a bowl covered with a cloth in a warm place. Then knead again. Cut it in equal pieces, knead again. Put the pieces in the bottoms of greased bread tins. Leave them covered until risen to the top of the tins. Then bake in a hot oven (220°C, 425°F, Mark 7) for 15 minutes. Reduce the heat to (190°C, 375°F, Mark 5) for 35 minutes. Cool the bread on a wire tray.

In little restaurants in the South of France they do a delicious fish soup flavoured and coloured with saffron. They bring it to the table in a vast brown pot, like something in which you might keep an aspidistra, ladling it out by the litre (2 pints), complete with spaghetti, chunks of carrot, and whole potatoes. There is also a brown jar of grated cheese left on the table for sprinkling in the soup. Filling? Very. But the grated cheese is delicious in a fish soup. Why do so few people do it here? Any British fishmonger will be delighted to let you have the heads, bones and skins left over from filleting sole and other luxury fish. They make excellent fish stock which, when cold, will set to a jelly.

Mediterranean Fish Soup

Frizzle a large, sliced onion and a chopped, garlic clove gently in a couple of tablespoons of olive oil in a saucepan with some sliced carrot, till the onion is almost melting and transparent but not brown. Add a litre (2 pints) of water, a thin piece of orange peel, some chopped parsley, a bay leaf, a teaspoon of paprika, some salt and a tin of peeled tomatoes. Then add your fish bones and trimmings together with a few of the more flavoursome looking fish from the shop – after all you must buy something! It could be whiting, gurnard, sprats, a couple of herrings or perhaps a mackerel or a little crab meat, it doesn't much matter. Conger eel, usually very cheap, makes marvellous fish soup, and the French say the black-skinned kind is the best. But you have to simmer it for about half an hour or it will be tough. Bring the soup to the boil and cook it over a fairly high heat for about 20 minutes. Add to this already well-flavoured stock the contents of a little packet of saffron soaked and mashed in half a teacup of hot water. Then strain the soup, pressing as much as you can of the vegetables and fish through the sieve.

Re-heat it and tip it into a large pot. This is eaten with chunks of crisp French bread rubbed with cut garlic and placed in each soup plate before the soup is ladled on top. There should also be a dish of grated cheese for sprinkling over it. When there is a lot of fish, French people sometimes serve this on a separate plate. With a bottle of wine and a large bowl of fresh fruit this makes what the French call a copious repast.

Cheese—Toasted Mostly

"Many's the long night I have dreamed of cheese – toasted mostly," said poor Ben Gunn after being marooned three years on Treasure Island, "and woke up again and here I were . . . You mightn't happen to have a piece of cheese about you now?"

Poor man, it is pathetic isn't it? To think of him sitting there all alone among the palm trees and mosquitoes and dreaming about food. Thinking, perhaps, of hot jacket potatoes squelching with cheese and melted butter, of cheese soufflés, and crumbly blue Wensleydale with rich fruit cake. He may even have dreamed of bacon and eggs and that ripe, nutty odour of grilled kidneys as it floats upstairs from the kitchen at breakfast time. Of lumps of Camembert and Gorgonzola.

Or perhaps he was thinking of that marvellous French *soupe à l'oignon* which was such a hot favourite in the old-fashioned Paris bistros. It is very filling and absolutely gorgeous, but I have never seen it on a desert island.

Soupe à l'Oignon

Melt 2 tablespoons of butter in a big saucepan and in it gently fry 2 or even 3 largish sliced onions. Put a lid on it so they go a nice golden blond and remain all soft and tender. Then add salt, pepper, a sprinkling of flour and 1 litre (2 pints) of water. Stir, bring it to the boil and just let it simmer for about 20 minutes.

Meanwhile cut a dozen small hunks of bread 3 cm (a good inch) thick. The best would be from one of those slender crisp French loaves. Toast them on one side, then, 3 minutes before the soup is ready, turn over the bread and put a thick slice of cheese on each piece and toast it until it begins to trickle down the sides. Put these in a soup tureen, pour your hot onion soup over the top and eat at once before the bread gets soggy. Cheddar cheese does very well in the soup but Gruyère, though expensive, is perhaps even better, as it goes into lovely stringy bits when it has melted. I can almost taste it now.

The nicest thing, after all, about the onset of autumn is that it does give you an appetite. And indeed, what could be better on a miserable misty evening than to sit round the fire in bedroom slippers eating toasted cheese. For the wickedly satisfying thing about it, too, is that cheese goes beautifully with any form of drink. Red wine, beer, stout, hot mulled plonk or what you will. So draw down the blinds, poke up the fire and gather round for cheese and chestnuts. Years ago the pubs used to do a superb toasted cheese thing dribbling with red wine and all hot and steaming.

Toasted Cheese

You toast a slice of bread on both sides then lay it in a plate before the fire, or in the warm oven. Pour a glass of red wine over it and let it soak the wine up in the warmth. Then cut some cheese very thin and lay it very thick over the bread (like you do in the *soupe à l'oignon*) and put it back in a very hot oven or under the grill and it will be toasted and browned almost at once. You should eat it as rapidly as possible.

Gnocchi alla Romana

Cheese Charlotte or *Gnocchi alla Romana* is one of those lovely simple Italian dishes which are very cheap to make. We often have it at home for supper and I am sure Ben Gunn would have enjoyed it too. First cook 100 g (4 oz) of semolina in a pan with a little boiling salted water until it is thick and smooth – thicker than for a semolina pudding. Add 25 g (1 oz) of grated cheese. Take it off the heat and stir in 2 eggs, mixing it thoroughly. Now pour the mixture on to a wide shallow dish in a layer about 1 cm (½ inch) thick, and let it get cold. Butter a pie dish or baking dish, then with your fingers roll the cooked semolina into little *gnocchi* – sort of tiny sausage things – or, if you like, just press out little rounds with the top of a sherry glass. Put them in your buttered pie dish with 100 g (4 oz) of melted butter, a sprinkling of salt and pepper and 100 g (4 oz) of grated cheese heaped over the top. Bake it in a moderate oven (180°C, 350°F, Mark 4) for about 30 minutes. If liked, it can be prepared in the morning, then just baked at dinner time.

Autumn Dinner Party

You could smell it really most of the afternoon. A rich, brown, thick sort of smell compounded of mushrooms, juniper berries, and hot grouse mingling with long, glistening chunks of onion which had been fried in butter.

There is something particularly satisfying about a grouse casserole. What is so pleasing about a casserole dish, however, is that you have so much longer to savour it in anticipation – a good two hours of rich, gamey odour seeping out of the kitchen, creeping darkly up the stairs, and greeting you at your door, all thick and alcoholic, when you come in after 6 o'clock. With a roast grouse it would be all over, bar the bones, in an hour at most for they take only about 20 minutes to cook.

Avocado Vinaigrette

We began with a very ripe avocado pear, half each and just with a tablespoon of olive oil, a dessertspoon of wine vinegar, a little coarse salt and freshly ground black pepper well mixed and poured into the hollow in the middle.

Grouse Casserole

In the middle of the morning I had put the grouse to soak in an old pudding basin with a good breakfast cup of red wine, a little salt and pepper and a few stalks of fresh parsley, thyme and rosemary from the garden. Dried herbs would do, though not quite so well. Then I put in about a dozen juniper berries. These are soft and black and about the size of peppercorns. You can get them from good grocers and delicatessen shops and though not essential they are very good in pâtés and game dishes. I also added about 100 g (4 oz) of ordinary raw, sliced mushrooms just for the look of the thing, but what gave the heavenly flavour to the finished dish was a little packet of dried Continental mushrooms called *steinpilze* from Bavaria which I put in at the same time. You can get these from good grocers and delicatessen shops. What I am talking about are those delicious *boletus edulis* or *cèpes* as the French call them, though they have no name in English. You can also get them here tinned in brine and fresh in season in some shops in Soho, as well as dried in packets. They are delicious in stews and casseroles and you can even use them in an omelette if you soak them first for about half an hour in a couple of tablespoons of warm water.

Then, at least 2 hours before dinner, I sliced and fried 2 large carrots, 2 onions, and a bit of garlic in about 2 tablespoons of butter in a heavy fireproof dish, gently so they went soft rather than brown. I dried the well-drained grouse and browned that all over, turned it on its back, laid three rashers of streaky bacon on its bosom and added the contents of the pudding basin, wine, mush-rooms, herbs and all.

Then I put a lid on the casserole and left it chunnering away quietly to itself in a very moderate oven for well over 2 hours till we were ready to eat. Just before serving I put the grouse on a hot dish with most of the casserole vegetables, then, to reduce the quantity of thick dark gravy and make it even better, I boiled it fiercely for a few minutes in the fireproof dish *stirring all the time* so that it got really strong and thick before pouring it over the bird. This we had garnished with watercress and flanked by the contents of a tin of unsweetened chestnut purée which I had heated gently in the oven with a little butter.

We finished the meal with a ripe smelly Gorgonzola cheese, oat-cakes and crisp celery and I also made two or three large crunchy apple fritters which we had sprinkled thickly with caster sugar. A bottle of *Châteauneuf du Pape* went beautifully with it.

Lord Nelson also Loved Marsala

It was Lord Nelson who made Marsala fashionable. He seems to have drunk a lot of it after the Battle of Aboukir when philandering in Naples with the wife of the British Ambassador, Lady Emma Hamilton. The luscious Emma Hamilton, that big plump girl with the Liverpool accent who wore no stays or drawers, and had been mistress of several fashionable Englishmen before she married Our Man in Naples, the elderly Sir William. Much painted by Romney, she was not only beautiful but an amusing, open-hearted and very passionate woman who was the love of Nelson's life.

As for the Marsala that they drank so much together, this was first shipped here at the end of the 18th century by two brothers from Liverpool, John and William Woodhouse who had originally gone to Sicily to buy raw materials for making soda. They suddenly realized that the local wines were very like those used for making port and sherry, saw the possibilities of making a rival drink, set up production and in 1773 exported the first Marsala to England. But it was Nelson who popularized it. When the HMS *Elizabeth* sailed from nearby Trapani in 1773 she took 60 barrels of it with her which he himself had ordered.

"Marsala wines are so good," he wrote, "that any gentleman may allow them on his table." He ordered quantities of it for the Fleet which may well have fought the Battle of Trafalgar on Marsala rather than naval rum. It is still known to the wine trade as "Bronte Marsala", after the Sicilian estate given him with a dukedom by the King of Naples.

But for a dinner with the Nelson touch you must serve *zabaione*, the delicately flavoured mixture of eggs and wine which is eaten hot in glasses and is recommended by Italian doctors as a restorative.

Zabaione

To make the *zabaione* allow 5 egg yolks, 4 tablespoons of sugar (the Italians generally use icing sugar) and 4 tablespoons of Marsala for about three people, whipping the yolks, wine and sugar together either in a pan over a low heat or in a large pudding basin which stands in a saucepan with hot water to come half way up it. Heat it gently, stirring all the time, until it froths up and thickens and increases to about four times the volume it was when you started. It only takes a few minutes, though if it boils it will curdle like an egg custard. But there is nothing difficult about it provided you think about what you are doing.

Marsala is still used a lot in Italian cooking and is particularly useful in the kitchen since it does not spoil if the bottle is left open a long time. A little Marsala is delicious stirred into a panful of fried chicken livers. Or poured into the familiar onion and tomato sauce one has with pasta.

Pollo alla Marsala

Cut a small chicken in pieces, dip these in seasoned flour and brown gently in butter or olive oil. Then simply pour in enough Marsala to cover it and simmer gently till tender. This may sound slightly extravagant but think how easy it is and how Emma Hamilton would have loved it.

Zabaione is also used for what is known in Italy as *Zuppa Inglese* or

"English soup". This has nothing to do with soup and nothing to do with the English either, unless it is the Italian version of some long forgotten Trifle or Victorian Tipsy Cake made, perhaps, to please the English aristocrats wintering in Italy in the early part of the 19th century.

Zuppa Inglese

Soak three layers of sponge cake in rum or brandy, sandwich them with *zabaione* and cover the top with whipped, sweetened cream about 2·5 cm (1 inch) thick, then decorate the top with crystallized fruit. If you like, the egg whites left over from the *zabaione* may be whipped stiffly and folded into the whipped cream to increase its volume.

English soup or no, some of the original English descriptions of the wine are still used in Sicily. S.O.M. – Superior Old Marsala, for instance. But the sweeter ones are now called after Garibaldi and some have his picture on the bottle. This is because, when Garibaldi and his Thousand were liberating Italy from the Bourbons in 1860, he too landed at Marsala in something of the atmosphere of a comic opera. When he arrived off Marsala two British men-of-war were standing off-shore to protect the British inhabitants "nearly all of whom were engaged in making Marsala". Garibaldi was then wildly popular in Britain and the women were all mad about him, for he was very good looking, and sedate English ladies used to wear bright red blouses copied from the shirts of his leaders. Scores of young English aristocrats joined his army incognito.

Anyway, to cut a long story short, the opposing Neapolitan warship *Stromboli* was finally persuaded that not only was the town full of British soldiers – and there were in fact half a dozen British officers eating ice-cream in a café – but that if they opened fire they might hit the Marsala factory. One shot did however enter Mr Woodhouse's wine establishment and nearly killed Mrs Harvey, the manager's wife . . . Later the *Times* correspondent of that day managed to interview General Garibaldi at his H.Q. He was standing in a group with fifteen or twenty followers "in what seemed like a gypsy encampment, with horses tethered beneath the trees, blankets and coats spread out amongst the boulders and on a smoking fire a huge pot full of meat and onions, beside the fire was a barrel of Marsala and a basket of bread. The staff were helping themselves to the food with their fingers and sharing the single pot from which they drank the Marsala." This must have been a version of the *Bistecca alla Marsala* still so popular in Sicily but made, of course, in larger quantities.

Bistecca alla Marsala

Take a fireproof dish, in it fry one or two large chopped onions and a large chopped garlic clove in 2 or 3 tablespoons of olive oil. Add 800 g (2 lb) of stewing steak cut in pieces. When this is brown stir in a little flour. Add 125 ml (¼-pint) of water, 125 ml (¼-pint) of Marsala and the contents of a small tin of tomato purée. Heat, stirring. Add salt and pepper and bring it gently to the boil. Put a lid on the dish and let it simmer for about 2 hours in a moderate oven (180°C, 350°F, Mark 4) until the meat is tender. Stir occasionally.

All About Walnuts

Nowadays there are really no English walnuts for we cut the trees down and sold the wood to make furniture years ago. Nobody seems to grow them now. The new season's crops from Sorrento and from California, however, appear here in November. One could go on cracking and eating them for hours, munching them with salt and some rather smelly Gorgonzola cheese, though I believe some people like them mixed with honey in thin brown bread and butter sandwiches.

Walnut Salad

They make a luscious salad. Prepare a lettuce as usual, washing the leaves and shaking them dry and tearing them apart with your fingers (for cutting a lettuce makes it go bitter and brown). Chop some shelled walnuts and mix them with a small carton of thick soured cream. Add salt and pepper, toss the lettuce in this at the last minute and add some very thin slices of Cox's orange pippins. This is lovely with roast chicken and chips instead of a hot vegetable.

Shelled walnuts mixed with cream cheese – or curd cheese – are delicious with a plate of cold ham. One can also add some sliced pineapple. The walnuts go perfectly with the soft creamy cheese. Recently in France I tasted one which had been garnished all over with halved walnuts, like a sponge sandwich, and it tasted as good as it looked.

Green walnuts picked in July and still in their outer casing are what we use for pickling – an old English speciality unknown abroad and superb with a thick ox-tail stew, as well as with a cold cut off the joint. Some of the old cooks used also to make them into ketchup laced with port and flavoured with anchovies. In the Balkans they bottle their halved green walnuts in a sticky syrup and eat them with Turkish coffee. You can buy these here sometimes in the supermarkets. They are very good on ice-cream or to garnish a rich gâteau and much cheaper than *marrons glacés*.

In some parts of France they still cook in walnut oil. It has a strange nutty flavour which is, perhaps, an acquired taste but is very good in salads. It is becoming rare now though as the oil is expensive and quickly goes rancid.

Hot Hungarian Walnut Soufflé

Cream 60 g (2½ oz) of butter and the yolks of 6 eggs with 50 g (2 oz) of caster sugar, flavoured with a little vanilla, till fluffy and stiff. Then, having ground 125 g (5 oz) of walnuts (shelled weight) either in the electric mixer or an ordinary mincer with fine plates, stir these into the mixture. Whip the egg whites so stiff the basin may be turned upside down without them falling out. Fold these gently into the soufflé mixture, tip it at once into a large, buttered soufflé dish, bake it at once in a pre-heated, moderate oven (180°C, 350°F, Mark 4) for 25–30 minutes. Run with it to the table and eat it at once with whipped cream or hot chocolate sauce.

Hungarian Walnut Gateau

This would be lovely for a party. Cream 8 egg yolks with 200 g (8 oz) of caster sugar. Add 200 g (8 oz) of ground walnuts, 2 tablespoons of soft white breadcrumbs, the grated rind of half a lemon and a tablespoon of rum. When it is well mixed fold in the very stiffly whipped whites of the 8 eggs. Turn it into two, large, buttered sandwich tins and bake in a pre-heated, moderate oven (180°C, 350°F, Mark 4) for 20–25 minutes. Do not open the oven door for the first 15 minutes. When cold it may be sandwiched with apricot jam and sprinkled on top with plain sifted icing sugar, or it may be sand-wiched with chocolate cream.

Chocolate Cream

Melt 50 g (2 oz) of plain, bitter, eating chocolate adding 100 g (4 oz) of butter and 90 g (3½ oz) of sugar. Off the fire beat in a raw egg and beat till smooth. Sandwich the cooled cake with it, spread the rest on top and sprinkle thickly with chopped walnuts. Chill the cake before serving.

When Nights are Drawing In

In this dark and dreary season of the year when the wet leaves lie dank and soggy in the gutters, the only thing is to go home, get out some saucepans and start thinking about food. For there are still bargains to be found in the shops if you are broad-minded about food and know what to look for. Jerusalem artichokes, for instance. Most people do not buy them because they are hell to peel and when boiled and served in a conventional white sauce have an unattractive grey appearance. But they are delicious sliced thinly – not peeled – in rounds and fried quickly in hot oil like chips.

Fresh mussels, cheap, nourishing and quick to cook are one of the most under-rated foods on the market. You can come home with a wet carrier bag full of them and have them grilled in snail butter – absolutely reeking with garlic, piping hot and delicious. 2 litres (4 pints) would be enough for 4 in this instance, and they are much cheaper than *escargots*. You think you would not like them? But have you ever tried them?

Mussels in Snail Butter

Rinse the mussels as usual in plenty of running water to get rid of the mud and sand. Scrape off the barnacles and whiskers with which they cling to the rocks. Throw away any which are broken or open, put the others in a wide shallow pan, with a spoonful of butter and a lid, over a fierce heat. Shake and stir them occasionally and in 5 to 6 minutes all should be open.

Mix your butter with pepper, chopped parsley and finely chopped garlic, proportions according to your taste. Remove one shell from each cooked mussel, stuff the one with the fish in it with the garlic butter, lay the stuffed mussels on a metal tray and put them under the griller just long enough for the butter to melt. Eat them at once with lots of crisp French bread. Delicious for starters and you can drink red wine with them.

The old game laws were so savage in this country and people were punished so cruelly for generations that I think we still have the idea at the back of our minds that game is something for the Lord of the Manor and is probably very expensive or terribly difficult to cook. Not a bit of it.

Hare is in season from 1st August to the end of February and is often extremely good value, apparently because a lot of people haven't the foggiest idea how to cook it. There is usually no need to buy a whole animal; butchers sell it cut up – just like rabbit. *Toasted Hare with Milk Gravy* is an old, country-house dish popular in Victorian England and well worth reviving. You will need the back – or saddle as they usually call it – in one piece, or if there are a lot of people, the back and hind legs (correctly known as a baron of hare) in one piece.

Toasted Hare with Milk Gravy

Stuff the hare with the forcemeat balls mixture described below and keep back the hare's liver for thickening the gravy. Sew or tie it up with coarse thread, put it in a fireproof dish big enough to take it lying flat. Brush the hare with melted butter and cover it with fat bacon rashers. Add 500 ml (1 pint) of milk and baste it with this at 20 minute intervals adding more as it reduces.

The whole secret of toasting hare is not letting the meat get dry. Some cooks baste the hare with beer or with bacon dripping. Bake it in a hot oven (190°C, 375°F, Mark 5) for 1½ hours for an old hare, or just under an hour for a leveret or young one. Ask the butcher which it is. Just before it is done put the liver in a little pan with water. Boil it up for about 3 minutes. Drain and purée it in the mixer. Add this to the milk which takes the colour of chocolate cream as it gets done. Mix 1 dessertspoon of flour with 2 tablespoons of cream, stir this gently into the gravy, heating it for a few minutes till the flour is cooked.

Serve this gravy on the meat dish with the hare placed on it, very hot, at the moment of serving. Do this with great care as it will have become rather crumbly. Hand round redcurrant or rowan jelly to eat with it. If you are having forcemeat balls and bacon rolls, these should be done in a separate tin in the oven. If liked, have hot, baked, jacket potatoes and oven-baked chicory or a garlicky tossed salad with it. Double the quantity of the forcemeat balls mixture if you want a lot of them.

Forcemeat Balls

To make the forcemeat balls mix 100 g (4 oz) of shredded suet with 50 g (2 oz) of finely diced bacon, 1 teaspoon of chopped parsley, 1 teaspoon of mixed herbs, the diced, thinly peeled rind of half a lemon and 150 g (6 oz) of soft white breadcrumbs. Add salt, a good pinch of grated nutmeg and a very little Cayenne pepper – which is very hot. Mix this thoroughly and add 2 beaten eggs. Use some of it to stuff the hare, roll the rest into little balls, bake them for about 20 minutes in a fireproof dish in the oven together with some rolled up rashers of bacon.

Heart to Heart with a Bummaree

"Hearts are depressed," said Ted Buttling, "and liver is little better . . ." We were sitting in the Cock Tavern in Smithfield Market eating cosy plates of hot buttered toast. The pub, which opens at 6.30 a.m. to serve drinks, juicy steaks and hot bacon sandwiches to bummarees and butchers, was full of very meaty personalities indeed.

Michael Caine was a porter here once, several of the men had carnations in their button holes and I saw one bloke in a delicately curved brown bowler with gloves, rolled umbrella, blue striped suit and waistcoat, looking like Steed in the *Avengers*, who turned out to be a meat porter in mufti having some toast after the night's work.

Nature often gets a bit red in tooth and claw at Smithfield. The wholesale market starts at 4 a.m. and packs up at about 1 o'clock. Though the pitchers bring the meat in about midnight the bummarees, or porters, cannot take it out without a permit before 5 a.m. Most of their conversation, when printable, seemed to me to be about horse racing.

"I've got up at 3 a.m.," said a man beside me in white overalls, "every day for the past 35 years. It's just as easy as getting up at seven." He would not let me give his name "for security reasons" but was wearing a Maurice Chevalier straw boater which, he said, protects the head from being bumped by turkeys and so on. "The brim is made extra thick with a serrated edge and provides protection from the hazards of the job. Meat hooks, swinging carcasses and all that. They make them for me specially." We had another round of toast. "Mother never lets me have lunch at the market," he said, pushing his boater to the back of his head. "She fixes me up some smoked salmon sandwiches or something decent, then we have our big meal at 5 o'clock, that's our life."

As for Ted Buttling, like most butchers he cannot understand why we do not buy more of the cheap and tasty cuts. "Forequarters of any kind has been sadly neglected for years," he said lugubriously, "and the housewife has stood back from hearts and livers. But why not have them in the fore part of the week like the old Mums used to? Why haven't they got a taste for it now?"

We sat there smacking our lips at the thought of steaming knuckle of pork in parsley sauce, sizzling hot, devilled trotters eaten with enough fiery English mustard to make your eyes water. Red flannel hash, faggots, and pease pudding, brains in black butter sauce and braised sliced lambs' hearts smothered in onions and with little forcemeat balls nestling in the thick brown gravy. Some of the more plebeian but tasty bits of the various animals are getting difficult to buy nowadays I told him. I have a hopeless passion for veal kidneys, for instance, done in a little dish in the oven, but you can hardly ever get them now – the restaurants buy them. And what about a nice, old-fashioned, ox-cheek stew, the kind of thing that was so rich and brown you could make a meal from the gravy alone? Since you can seldom get it now we settled for a great bubbling basin of stewing steak simmered in beer with bacon. Even the smell is nourishing.

"Since 1954 and the de-control of meat," Ted went on patiently, "it has been a troubled period; everyone's got steak minded. There's been a bit more money in the purse so both husband and wife have gone for the lamb chops and forgotten the beautiful succulent scrags and middles. And the breast of lamb boned and rolled. Wonderful families have been brought up on this through generations!"

I hadn't the heart to tell him that when I bought a shoulder of lamb from my favourite country butcher a few weeks back he *gave* me a huge piece of scrag as a present. "To flavour the gravy," he smiled, "nobody wants them and if you don't have it I shouldn't know what to do with it . . ." Now scrag is really just a lot of bones joined together by meat but if you are in a bit of a thing with the housekeeping money you could add some breast of lamb and make it into a smashing curry. Where it is really superb, however, is in a whopping great basin of first-rate, nourishing soup with enough for second and third helpings.

Devilled Trotters

You want some of these cold, boiled, split pig's trotters like the crubeens they have in Dublin pubs. Dip them in melted butter, then in breadcrumbs with cheese and a pinch of Cayenne pepper. Grill them gently for about 20 minutes turning them so they brown all over without letting them burn. Eat them with lots of mustard all piping hot in your fingers.

Beef in Beer

Brown 600 g (1½ lb) of stewing steak and 200 g (8 oz) of diced streaky bacon. Add 2 big sliced onions, a chopped leek and let them colour lightly in dripping. Stir in a little flour then add a pint of beer, preferably light ale, stirring it into the meat. Add salt, pepper, mixed herbs and 400 g (1 lb) of chopped carrots. Bring to the boil and simmer gently for 2½ hours, or cook it, covered, in a moderate oven (180°C, 350°F, Mark 4) for about 2½ hours. Serve sprinkled with chopped parsley.

Butcher's Broth

Put 600–800 g (1½–2 lb) of scrag or neck of mutton in a pan with 2 litres (4 pints) of cold water and a little salt. Skim when it boils. Simmer for 1 hour. Then add 2 chopped carrots, 2 chopped onions and a piece of turnip. Simmer covered for 30 minutes. Add a small, coarsely chopped cabbage or cauliflower, simmer for another 30 minutes till everything is tender. Take out the bones leaving the meat. Add a little chopped parsley and more seasoning if necessary. If liked a packet of frozen peas can be heated in the soup shortly before serving.

Sweetbreads have a most delicate flavour and are still comparatively cheap, but most people haven't the faintest idea how to cook them so they are mostly sold to the catering trade.

To Prepare Sweetbreads

First (and whatever the final recipe), you put the sweetbreads to soak in a basin of cold water for a couple of hours. Then tip them into a pan of cold salted water, bring it to the boil and simmer them for about 2 minutes. Drop them in cold water then strip off any fat and the kind of skinny bits which are apt to be a bit chewy. None of this takes long and you could do it hours before you actually cook the sweetbreads.

Fried Sweetbreads

The simplest way to serve them after boiling is just to slice them, shake them in seasoned flour and fry them with bacon. This is delicious. If you like you could garnish the dish with a bit of watercress and a heap of sauté potatoes.

Sweetbreads in Lemon Sauce

Buttery new potatoes or plain boiled rice would go perfectly with this. Just sizzle about 300 g (12 oz) of sliced sweetbreads (prepared as before) very gently with 100 g (4 oz) of sliced mushrooms in about 75 g (3 oz) of hot butter. It will smell delicious, but restrain yourself, we have not finished yet. Before the sweetbreads get actually brown stir in 1½ tablespoons of flour, a little salt and pepper and a good pinch of nutmeg. Then gradually add 375 ml (¾-pint) of hot stock – water and a chicken bouillon cube – and heat, stirring, to make a nice smooth sauce. Add a bay leaf and a strip of lemon peel if you have any, then let it simmer for about 20 minutes, stirring occasionally. Beat up an egg with the juice of a lemon and stir a little of the hot sauce into it. Then tip the whole thing back into the pan and heat, gently, stirring. This thickens the sauce and gives it a subtle and elusive flavour. But do not let it boil or the egg will scramble.

Vol-au-Vent

If there is any left over it makes a perfect filling for those puff pastry cases called vol-au-vents. One can get them ready cooked from some bakers, or quick frozen in packets from supermarkets and grocers. Let these thaw for about half an hour, brush over with milk and bake in a very hot oven (220°C, 425°F, Mark 7) for about 15 minutes before filling.

Winter

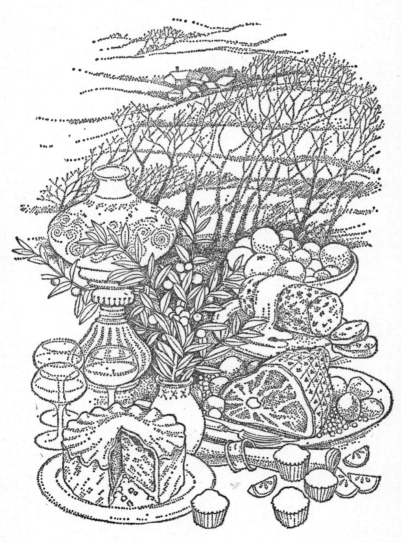

Hunting the Truffle

It was just after 6 a.m. and dark when I arrived at Asti truffle market. The stallholders in the main market were setting fire to old boxes to keep warm. We hurried off through the silent streets. You knew you were getting warm by the smell of the men walking towards the café. Everybody reeked of truffles. There were men inside drinking those small cups of very strong coffee that make your hair stand on end. But no other women.

The districts around Alba and Asti in Northern Italy are famous for white truffles, a delicious kind of fungus that fetches well over £50 per kilo (£20 per lb) in Italian shops. They grow wild underground in autumn and truffle hunters dig them up with the help of specially trained little dogs which sniffle them out.

The Italians do not cook them, they grate them raw on to a risotto or pasta or a meat salad or turkey – on almost anything. The head waiter brings in the truffle, which is a sort of greyish dusty beige, not white at all really. He has a stainless steel grater and he grates it on the meat, or whatever, in thin slices.

They look like bits of cardboard and have an extraordinary smell. Worse than garlic. An awful smell like strong cheese, which you nevertheless enjoy.

Truffles are best and most expensive when large and compact. Their shape depends on the earth – if it is stony or not. In Asti they had them wrapped in newspaper, or old table-cloths. I saw some extraordinary wrinkled faces over the café tables – all in felt hats and very secretive. They eat in their hats, and at home just push them to the back of their heads.

My friend Giuseppe Vivalde, a truffle merchant from Narsole, who gets up at 3 a.m. to go to market, bought from three people. There were small scales in the corner and about twenty buyers. The rest were selling and somebody told me there were about 120 k (300 lb) in the market that morning. The haggling was all done by 7.30. The buyer decides the price and the selling is mostly done by mime, with truffles fished out of pockets, offered, pushed away in disgust, and prices laughed to scorn.

Truffle merchants earn a lot of money. I spoke to Franco Parato, a young, thin, horsy-looking truffle merchant just off to Turin to sell them. He had an Alfa Romeo. I also met a man who last year found a truffle bigger than a grapefruit weighing more than 700 g (1¾ lb).

Everyone dreams of finding a perfectly shaped one of such fabulous size as to make his fortune. They are very secretive about where the truffles are, which is not surprising since they are worth so much, and there are frightful disputes about whose land they are actually on.

In October, at the start of the season, everybody goes truffle hunting at dawn so as not to be seen, but at this time of year the ground frost destroys the early scent. So it was after an enormous lunch in Santa Vittoria d'Alba that we all piled into a little red motor car to go truffle hunting in the hills above.

The smell of truffles was, well, deafening. Giuseppe Vivalde held his hat over my eyes so I wouldn't be dazzled by the sun but I managed to see the breath-taking view of the Alps and the Monte Rosa in the distance, round the edges of the brim.

We contacted our truffle hunter Luigi Allessandro and his dog, Moretto, near the Barolo vineyards. They produce an excellent dry, velvety wine, red and one of the best in Italy.

Moretto is a little eight-year-old black and white mongrel with a marvellous nose. He works on an empty stomach and Signor Allessandro gives him a bit of bread soaked in wine to keep him warm. These dogs are mostly mongrels and very valuable – there is a kind of canine university in Roddi where they train them.

Signor Allessandro said he had found about 1 k 200 g (3 lb) of truffles, mostly under oak trees. He puts the earth back carefully afterwards and keeps a note of the time and place but tells nobody. Next year he comes back and there are more. The dog is no good without the man who remembers the place.

We dug up a £10 one which looked like a potato or part of somebody's foot. Moretto nearly goes mad to get them and you have to dig too, quickly, so he doesn't damage them with his claws. We both scrambled like mad, Moretto with his feet, I with a steel truffle pick. We found another in a vineyard. You get them sometimes under lime trees, even under the street. There is a house near Alba where a man finds enormous truffles under the path every year. The owners get furious as they can never trace them.

Later the little dog dug up a black truffle, like the ones from Perigord, under some hazel trees but nobody thought much of it and part of it was thrown away. I did not dare to pick it up. When I said these were expensive in France they looked amazed. "Must use them for decoration," somebody said, "a black olive would do just as well."

That night we went back to the hotel and I had more truffles grated over a gorgeous, white-wine risotto which, between you and me, is really almost as good plain.

White Risotto

Fry a small, finely chopped onion in a big saucepan in 30 g (a good ounce) of butter. When golden add 75 g (3 oz) per person of long-grained, preferably Italian, rice, stirring to coat it with butter. Pour in a big tumbler of dry, white wine – plain or sparkling – simmer till the wine has almost disappeared. Now begin adding clear chicken or turkey broth which you have ready simmering in a second pan. Add a cupful at a time, a second if it all evaporates. It takes about 1 litre (2 pints) for 300 g (12 oz) of rice, but add a little more wine at the end if the stock has not been enough, stirring to stop the rice sticking to the pan bottom. Before serving add another 25 g (1 oz) of butter and 25 g (1 oz) freshly grated Parmesan cheese. Serve more butter and grated Parmesan cheese with it to sprinkle over the top. Fried chicken livers are almost as good as truffles with it.

Flaming Trout

For this the waiter turned out all the lights in the dining-room. Fry the trout lightly in butter, open them, remove the backbones, fill the space with a paste of egg yolks mixed with tinned tomato purée. Lay the fish in a fireproof dish on a bed of thyme twigs (in packets from good grocers). Cover them with more thyme twigs. Put it in a very hot oven (230°C, 450°F, Mark 8) for about 10 minutes to finish cooking and ignite the thyme. Pour warm brandy over before the flame dies and set it on the table.

Christmas Pudding

Christmas puddings are made, traditionally, on Stir Up Sunday around November 21st, when the Collect in church begins with the words: "Stir up we beseech Thee, O Lord . . ." They improve with keeping, like good wine, and seem to become richer and more delicious as the mixture matures. Some families make them a year ahead to eat the following Christmas, and many cooks make enough Christmas pudding in Autumn to have enough left for Easter Sunday as well. This is a well-tried recipe for a rich, old-fashioned, Christmas pudding made with carrots and brown ale.

You need 200 g (8 oz) self-raising flour, ¼-teaspoon salt, 1 teaspoon freshly grated nutmeg, 1 teaspoon mixed spice, 50 g (2 oz) ground almonds, 300 g (12 oz) fresh white breadcrumbs, 300 g (12 oz) sugar, 400 g (1 lb) currants, 400 g (1 lb) sultanas, 400 g (1 lb) stoned raisins, 100 g (4 oz) chopped mixed peel, 300 g (12 oz) shredded or fresh-grated suet, 100 g (4 oz) carrots, the juice and grated rind of a lemon, 125 ml (¼-pint) brown ale or stout, 6 eggs.

Sift the flour, salt, nutmeg, spice and ground almonds into a bowl. Rub the bread through a sieve to make crumbs, stir them with the sugar into the flour mixture.

Mix the currants, sultanas, stoned raisins and chopped mixed candied peel with the suet. Wash, dry and grate the carrots into it, and add to the flour mixture, stir in the grated lemon rind.

Mix well and thoroughly with a large wooden spoon. Get the family to help you stir the Christmas pudding and wish. Then let the basin stand, covered, in a cool place overnight. Next day stir in the beer and strained lemon juice, stir well and mix thoroughly. Beat up the eggs and mix them in with your hand.

Butter the pudding basins and fill to within 2·5 cm (1 inch) of the top, to leave room for the pudding to rise. 750 ml to 1 litre (1½-2 pint) pudding basins are a convenient size for modern families as they yield 8 ample portions. Cover the basins with 2 thicknesses of greased foil pleated across the middle and tied down firmly with string. Then, if liked, cover each with a pudding cloth, knotting the ends over to make a handle. Boil them on a rack in the saucepans with boiling water to come half way up the basins, cover with a lid.

When topping up what has boiled away see that the water is boiling when poured in. Boil the puddings for 7 hours and then a further 2-3 hours on Christmas Day.

When cooked, let them cool, then cover them with fresh clean foil and pudding cloths if used. Store in a dry place.

To flame and serve a Christmas Pudding

Do not forget the lucky sixpences, if you have any.

To flame the pudding the spirits must be warm or they will not light. It is rather like starting a car in cold weather. I find it easiest to pour a little rum or whisky into a frying pan, warm it and pour this over the pudding as I light it.

Sauce for a Christmas Pudding

Serve whipped sweetened cream, or *Zabaione* (see page 86) or what is known as *Senior Wrangler* or *Hard Sauce* with the pudding. An excellent, no trouble but rather expensive, sauce is made by pouring part of a bottle of Dutch Advocaat on the pudding as it is served.

Senior Wrangler or Hard Sauce

This is made by creaming 150 g (6 oz) of unsalted butter with 150 g (6 oz) of sifted icing sugar and beating in three or four tablespoons of brandy or other spirits. If one does this too fast it curdles.

Spiced Beef

Spiced Beef, the traditional Irish Christmas delicacy, is that joint you see rolled in cloves, nutmeg and brown sugar and tied up with holly and red ribbon, in Irish butchers' shops at Christmas. Forgotten here for a hundred years, it was the height of fashion in Victorian England. And no wonder! It is delicious with cold ham and turkey. We have it cold with hot, jacket potatoes and pickled walnuts on Boxing Day.

To spice your own 1 k 200 g (3 lb) of beef brisket or silverside, rub it well with a mixture of ½-teaspoon each of ground cloves, ground nutmeg and allspice, 2 tablespoons of brown sugar, a pinch of thyme, pepper, crushed bay leaf, a bit of chopped onion, 200 g (8 oz) of coarse salt, 1 tablespoon of saltpetre (from the chemist's shop). Leave it two days, then pour 1 tablespoon of treacle over it. Rub in the spicy mixture every day for a week. Tie it up with string, cover it with warm water, simmer gently for 3 hours. Nicest cold.

Roast Beef

The great thing about Christmas dinner is that you should enjoy it. My idea for a lovely meal would be under-done Roast Beef, thickly carved and cooked on the bone, with a good burgundy or a gutsy red wine from the Rhone valley.

It is what people had for Christmas until about 100 years ago. 1 k 200 g–1 k 600 g (3–4 lb) sirloin of beef on the bone would do 6–7 people nicely, but without enough to have cold later. The best part is the chump end with the undercut – on the bone it looks like a huge cutlet. When it is boned and rolled it is easier to carve, but it is also more expensive and does not taste so good. So bone up on your carving!

The beef, beer and bread of England have been famous since Tudor times, and in the 19th century those who could buy it stuffed themselves with beef in vast quantities. "Beef makes boys into men, beef nerves our navvies, the bowmen who won Creçy and Agincourt were beef fed," they used to say a bit optimistically, since most people could not afford it. The Roast Beef of Old England was looked on as something very manly, very British, and regarded with much the same reverence as some now have for cricket.

If you want something a little cheaper, Wing Rib – the next cut to sirloin – looks like a giant cutlet and is delicious, especially easy to serve. It is what many butchers have for Sunday dinner.

Roast Beef

Buy it on the bone and you are sure it is the real thing. Sprinkle the beef with pepper and powdered mustard if you like, but do not add salt till after it's cooked. I roast it 15 minutes per 400 g (1 lb) and

15 minutes over, in a hot oven (200°C, 400°F, Mark 6) because I like it red and juicy in the middle. Some people prefer it roasted 20 minutes per 400 g (lb) and 20 minutes over. When it's done, put it on a warm dish, let it stand 15 minutes by the open stove to set and become ready to carve. It is best when carefully basted. Don't make that nasty thick gravy, but try the thin kind flavoured with sherry – it is excellent with any roast.

A good Beef Gravy

I pour the surplus fat out of the roasting tin into a dripping pot, then I stir a glass of sherry or whatever we are drinking into the tin, heating and stirring up the brown bits in the bottom to make a delicious boozy gravy.

Parsnips are traditional with roast beef, and cheap too. They can be peeled and roasted beside the joint with the potatoes, and served as well as the sprouts, Yorkshire pudding and freshly made English mustard.

Buying a Turkey

Luxury models are the small, fresh, hen turkeys. Usually dearer than the tom or cock turkey, they are juicier, with smaller bones and bigger breasts. Weight: 3–7 kilo (8–16 lb) with a sort of football-shaped body and small legs. Fresh tom turkeys weigh 5–8 kilo (14–20 lb) with a high breast bone, thicker neck and big gobble-de-gook head.

To work out the size of a fresh turkey remember they are sold according to the undressed weight, which includes the innards, head and everything. When ready for table it will be a much lighter bird. Frozen oven-ready turkeys, however, are sold according to their dressed weight per kilo (lb); so that a fresh undressed turkey of 5 kilo (12 lb) is about equal to a frozen oven-ready one of 4 kilo (9 lb). Allow about 300 g (¾-lb) frozen oven-ready bird per person. A 2–3 kilo (6–8 lb) bird gives roughly 6–10 servings, a 3–4 kilo (8–12 lb) turkey 10–12 servings, a 4–7 kilo (12–16 lb) turkey 15–24 servings.

The turkey's skin should be white – avoid those with reddish skins or birds with blackish specks or a scarred and battered look, for they have been too long in storage.

Frozen turkeys must be thawed completely before cooking. It takes about 48 hours in a cool larder to thaw a big bird. Remove the bag of giblets when it is sufficiently thawed to do so.

Cooking the Turkey

A small fresh turkey, or capon, or farmhouse roasting chicken, "blistered with raspings" in the traditional manner is one of my specialities. I revived the old recipe from a manuscript cookery book some years ago and everybody loves it. This is the dish that, as I discovered later, was well liked in Jane Austen's England and popular in Scotland during a great part of the 19th century. The bird comes out of the oven looking as if it were wearing a short fur coat. The outside is all crisp and shaggy, with the roasted cheese and breadcrumbs. It isn't a gimmick, the whole thing looks absolutely delightful when brought to table garnished with crisp bacon rolls, forcemeat balls, a string of sausages and the Liver and Lemon Sauce fashionable about the same time.

Turkey with Raspings

Sew or skewer it up, trussing the legs, and then butter the bird all over with about a breakfast cup of poultry dripping or 200 g (8 oz) of softened butter. Ordinary dripping will *not* do, as it will spoil the delicate flavour of the bird.

Sprinkle the bird with salt and pepper and roast it 20 minutes per 400 g (1 lb) and 20 minutes over, in a moderate oven (180°C, 350°F, Mark 4) with a piece of foil laid loosely across the breast. Pour a glass of white wine or water under the bird and add another while cooking, if it has largely evaporated. Baste it occasionally. To see if it is cooked, thrust a fork firmly into the thigh, if the gravy runs clear, it is done. If, as sometimes happens, there is a reduction of gas pressure or electric power on Christmas Day it will throw the timing out.

Meanwhile grate enough white bread for 1½ breakfast cups of

crumbs and mix with 3 heaped tablespoons of grated cheese. About 15 minutes before the bird is done, take it out of the oven and let it cool for a bit. Increase the oven heat to really hot (220°C, 425°F, Mark 7). Then pour the fat from the tin over the bird repeatedly with a spoon.

Coat it all over with the crumbs and the cheese, patting them on the buttery thighs with your fingers. Pour on a bit more fat gently and more crumbs. Return the bird to the really hot oven to brown.

Celery Stuffing for Turkey

For the stuffing, put 2 breakfast cups of finely chopped celery in a pan with 2 tablespoons of butter, salt, pepper and a finely chopped onion. Let them simmer with a lid on till limp, not brown. Stir in 2 cups of soft white breadcrumbs; let these fry lightly before stuffing the bird.

The old *Liver and Lemon Sauce* has a most clean and delicate flavour and would go with roast or boiled poultry. There were many variations of it in the 18th century when it was sometimes known as *Hanover Sauce*. I cannot imagine why it was ever forgotten.

Liver and Lemon Sauce

While the turkey is cooking, poach its liver in 375 ml (¾-pint) of stock from the giblets, or water and a bouillon cube. Peel a lemon thinly and cut the peel in strips as for marmalade. Mince or chop the liver as finely as possible, do not purée it. Melt 2 tablespoons of butter in a little pan. Stir in 1½ tablespoons of flour, then gradually add the stock, heating and stirring. Season it with pepper, salt and grated nutmeg. Add the lemon peel, the minced turkey liver, lastly the juice of the lemon.

The turkey will look absolutely charming garnished with old English forcemeat balls and crisp bacon rolls.

Old English Forcemeat Balls

While the turkey is cooking simmer 100 g (4 oz) of sliced mushrooms in a little butter then tip and mix them into 500 ml (1 pint) of white crumbs, some salt, pepper, 1 teaspoon of grated lemon rind, the yolks of 2 eggs, 40 g (a good 1½ oz) of butter and any mushroom juice. The mixture should be fairly firm. Roll it into little balls with floury hands. Fry them, put them round the bird with the bacon rolls.

If you have any foil to spare make two strips into little shaggy frills to go round the turkey's ankles.

In the old days a complete chain of chipolata sausages – rather like the kind of thing used by pantomime comedians when chased by Dick Whittington's cat – was laid across the breast of the bird before serving, when it was traditionally known as an Alderman in Chains – whether or not it was wearing a short fur coat! Prick and bake the sausages with the bacon rolls in a separate tin for the last 30 minutes.

Sprouts with Cheese and Onion

Roast potatoes and sprouts, fried with cheese and onion as they do them in Brussels, would go perfectly with it. Clean the sprouts, leave them in cold salted water to freshen. Cook them in a *little* boiling salted water for a few minutes. Remove and drain while still crisp. Fry a couple of rashers of diced bacon and a large grated onion in 50 g (2 oz) of butter. Toss the well drained sprouts in it, fry them until just golden. Serve sprinkled with a little grated cheese.

Hot Roast Gammon

Hot Roasted Gammon or forehock would go well with a small turkey and be good cold on Boxing Day, or it could be served hot on Christmas Eve with jacket potatoes, broccoli and spiced fruit pickles. Half a gammon weighs about 3 kilo (8 lb). A boned, rolled forehock, which can either be baked or boiled, weighs 800 g–1 k 200 g (2–3 lb) and is weight for weight a cheaper cut.

Roast Forehock of Bacon

To roast a forehock of bacon or a gammon soak it 24 hours in cold water. Wrap it in foil, bake it 15 minutes per 400 g (lb) and 15 minutes over in a moderate oven (180°C, 350°F, Mark 4). Twenty-five minutes before the end, rip off the skin, cut the fat in diamonds or squares, and glaze it with orange.

Orange Glaze for Gammon or Forehock

Mix 150 g (6 oz) of soft brown sugar with the grated rind and juice of an orange and the grated rind of a lemon. Spread this on the fat about 25 minutes before it comes out of the oven.

Omelette Soufflé Noël

An Omelette Soufflé Noël is as light as snow, full of mincemeat and delicious. For four people, first butter a long shallow fireproof dish, one of those oval copper sauté pans looks charming when brought to the table. Sprinkle it all over the inside with caster or icing sugar, spread some mincemeat, laced with whisky or rum or other spirits, on the bottom. Beat four egg yolks with 200 g (8 oz) of caster sugar and a pinch of salt until pale straw coloured. Add 2 tablespoons of thick cream. Whip the four egg whites so stiff that the basin may be turned upside down without them falling out, then fold them delicately into the yolks. Pile the mixture into the dish in a long hump. Smooth the top with a knife blade and make some cuts in it. Bake your omelette soufflé *at once* in a moderate oven (180°C, 350°F, Mark 4) for 20 minutes so that the omelette rises and develops in volume. At the end sprinkle it with sifted icing sugar. Turn the oven to maximum hot and put it back to brown the sugar on top. It must be served immediately it comes out of the oven. On the way to the dining-table pour warm whisky or other spirits over it, set light to it and serve it flaming.

Mrs Charlie Smirke's Cold Turkey Salad

This would be an excellent way of serving some of the cold bird on Boxing Day. This is a recipe that I had from the wife of the famous jockey some years ago. It was a feature of the cold buffet party they always had at their house near Epsom on Derby Day – but it would be just as good at Christmas.

You just slice the cooked turkey removing the skin, then cut the slices into thin slivers almost as fine as the peel in coarse-cut marmalade. Then coat them in thick cream mixed with a little lemon juice, salt and pepper, a few capers and tiny chunks of cucumber. It looks pretty on a big meat dish decorated with watercress, hard-boiled eggs and anchovies.

A Simple Chocolate Mousse

This would be very useful during the New Year holiday. Just grate 40 g (1½ oz) plain slab chocolate per person into a basin. Then heat this over a pan of boiling water till it is soft. Separate the yolk and white of one egg per person. Stir the lightly beaten egg yolks into the melted chocolate with one heaped teaspoon of instant coffee per person. Then, having whipped the egg whites absolutely stiff in the mixer, stir these in gently. Pour it into little individual pots or into something like a soufflé dish and leave it for 3 hours or longer in a cool place, not in the fridge. You can have cream with it.

Bitter Seville Oranges

It is a widely held belief among some women journalists that only lunatics make marmalade. I dare say this is a delusion like so much else. The fact remains that if ever anyone gives recipes for it, however orthodox, an unusually large number of women seem to write to say they have got caught up in the peel, lost their nerve or have got into some other involved emotional marmalade hook-up. One woman once rang me at the office to say she'd got the oranges in the pan, was now utterly confused and hoped I would talk to her until she got her courage back. Well I did. I read an early copy of Mrs. Beeton to her in a low calm voice rather in the manner of someone in an airport control tower talking down an aircraft in thick fog.

Now you can buy jars of perfectly good homemade marmalade at the Women's Institute stalls and in those small country tea shops where they also make their own drop scones and Madeira cake, but Seville oranges can be put to other saner uses. They are delicious with roast tame or wild duck, so here are a few quick recipes.

Wild Duck with Orange

Teal, those tiny wild ducks about as big as a pigeon (if you can lay your hands on any) should be roasted with a split orange or a whole peeled tangerine inside them. Butter the bird all over, sprinkle it with salt and pepper, roast it in a tin with its own giblets for about 20 minutes in a hot oven (200°C, 400°F, Mark 6) basting it with butter and orange juice mixed.

Wild duck, by which I mean widgeon or mallard, are a bit bigger and should be cooked for 30–35 minutes in a hot oven (200°C, 400°F, Mark 6) with the heat reduced slightly at half time. Two birds are generally allowed for four people. Orange salad goes very well with them.

Aylesbury Duck with Orange Sauce

A nice domestic duck is just about enough for four people but won't do more, unless you are a conjuror. Take out the giblets. Don't bother to stuff it, rub it with salt and pepper, put a bit of fresh sage if you have any, inside it. Stand it on a rack in a roasting tin with the giblets below. Pour the contents of a tin of orange juice (not squash) together with the juice of 3 Seville oranges or 2 sweet oranges and 1 lemon over the duck. Roast it for about an hour and a half in a moderate oven (180°C, 350°F, Mark 4). Baste it from time to time with the fruit juice.

Cut the rind of the oranges in thin strips without any of the pith and boil them for 2 minutes. One thing about roast duck is that there is a lot of fat. I pour this off at half time and keep it, not only for making savoury pastry, for which it is delicious, but to smear all over those rather dry broiler chickens before roasting. When cooked, keep the duck warm while you stir the orange peel into the juices in the pan together with a teaspoonful of cornflour moistened with a drop of water. Heat, stirring, letting the sauce boil for a few moments and thicken before pouring it over the duck.

If you want to get away from the misery of carving just cut the bird into four with poultry or dressmaking scissors in the kitchen before serving. Serve garnished with watercress.

Bitter oranges were the first to be grown in Europe. The sweet orange, what Spaniards call the Valencia or China orange, arrived much later from the Far East. At first the bitter orange trees were just grown for the lovely scented orange blossom used for making perfume. Even now in flower-producing areas the oranges are sometimes just dumped in the rivers as no one has heard of marmalade. The blossoms are also used for orange flower water, a sweetly-scented liquid still popular in provincial France for flavouring puddings and cakes. You can buy it here quite cheaply from old-fashioned chemists and Cypriot grocers. It makes a very nice flavouring for a rice pudding or baked custard. And in Seville, apart from selling us the oranges for marmalade, they preserve great wrinkled black olives lusciously in bitter orange juice.

French Orange Conserve

Of course there must be scores of old family recipes for marmalade each a little different, some thick and dark and chunky, others clear as a stained-glass window. One very old French way of making it has whole orange segments and bits of peel floating in a rather thin golden syrup. It's a bit sticky for breakfast in bed. But gorgeous as a cake filling. Or piled into champagne glasses to eat with whipped cream or a lemon water ice. It also goes deliciously with roast gammon, cold ham and hot roast pork.

Weigh out 600 g (1½ lb) of caster sugar to every 400 g (1 lb) of bitter Seville oranges. Cut the peel in four, without damaging the fruit below, and strip the peel from the pith. Soak it for 24 hours in slightly salty water. Scrape the pith off the peeled oranges too, and divide them into sections getting out the pips without destroying the thin skin. Put the orange sections in a basin with layers of sugar and leave for 24 hours, when they will be swimming in a fragrant yellow syrup in which you cook the fruit. Boil the drained peel for about 2 hours in a pan of unsalted water with the lid on. If it feels tender when bitten it is done. Chop it into strips.

Put the layers of fruit, peel and all the syrupy juice in the preserving pan, heat it gently, don't stir for fear of damaging the oranges.

Shake the pan a bit until all the sugar melts and gradually goes liquid as the fruit weeps. Then bring it gently to the boil and boil till setting point is reached. It is important not to overcook the fruit which, when done, should be almost intact, well rounded and swimming like little goldfish in abundant amber jelly. It is rather thinner than English breakfast marmalade but I think it is absolutely marvellous.

Spanish Oranges in Syrup

Have you ever tasted that Spanish orange salad thing? You never saw it anywhere a few years ago, now it is on all the fashionable restaurant trolleys. It is at its most luscious, I suppose, when prepared with those small, deep-red, blood oranges.

You allow one each. Peel them whole without the pith or anything, just the naked flesh. Cut all the white pith off some of the orange peel too, then cut the peel into strips as one does for marmalade. For 6–8 portions heat 400 g (1 lb) of caster sugar gently in 250 ml (½-pint) water stirring until it melts. Then bring it to the boil and go on boiling, stirring occasionally, until in a few minutes you have a thickish syrup. Add the strips of orange peel and go on cooking it until it has almost caramelized. Then, when cold, add a little Cointreau or Grand Marnier or Orange Curaçao (mini bottles will do). Pour it over the oranges and serve them chilled, with cream if you like. They are the perfect end to a really rich meal and especially fragrant and delicious if left for 24 hours to mingle their flavours with that of the syrup.

A Magnificent Tripe

It was a grey gritty day when I was last in Lyon some years ago. The streets are paved with the same grey stone setts or *pavés* as they were in Manchester in my childhood. There's plenty of brass there too, though it's a silk not a cotton town and the place is absolutely crammed with famous restaurants. In Lyon you can get some of the best cooking in the whole of France.

La Voûte is a small obscure place with a tiny entrance near the Pont Bonaparte, but very jolly. Everybody knows Léa, the owner, who is a humourist as well as an impassioned cook. A magnificent blonde, with a table napkin tied round her neck when I saw her, she wears it as a sort of scarf with her expensive little black number, with enormous effect. She kisses most of the old customers.

There were baked pears, purple with red wine, heaped up on a platter on the bar counter. Masses of local cheese. *Saint Marcellin, Bleu Bresse,* that lovely thing rolled in dried grape pips, and an unusual local one called *la Cervelle de Canut,* which is whipped up with garlic and pepper. She keeps it in a kind of earthenware flowerpot thing to protect it from the air.

"I adore cooking, it's a passion," Léa tells you in that city of passionately involved cooks, ". . . my great pleasure." She does lots of very old almost forgotten dishes, likes long slow simmered cooking *" la cuisine mijottée"* as she told me and she does most things in stages like the *marmalade d'oranges* which I tasted at stage 2 – for her famous marmalade cake which was taking her nearly a week to make. It looks absolutely nothing on the outside but tastes marvellous. We all ate bits of pudding, passing the pieces round to one another at the different tables and marvelling at the flavour. Whether it was even better this week than last.

Mackerel in White Wine

My companion and I began the meal with ice cold mackerel done in white wine. It is a classic French dish popular throughout France and of a limpid simplicity, if you have the right ingredients. Léa cooks them whole, without the heads, and splits them at your table.

Slice a lemon thinly into a large pan, with 4 thinly sliced large carrots, 1 large peeled thinly sliced onion. Add 2 bay leaves, 2 sprigs of thyme, 4 cloves, 8 black peppercorns, 500 ml (1 pint) of water and 250 ml (½-pint) of dry white wine, and some salt.

Bring it slowly to the boil and let it simmer for 30 minutes. Put 6 small mackerel, cleaned and without the heads, into a wide shallow fireproof dish. Pour the hot liquid and vegetables over them and cook them for 10–15 minutes, or until they flake easily with a fork. Serve them chilled in their liquor.

Most of her customers are old friends, and she has a black poodle named Monsieur Nico, whom, you feel, in that atmosphere is probably something of a gourmet himself. " *C'est une personnalité,*" as she says.

What with the *Caneton de Louhane fourré au foie gras*, the crayfish in cream, the *saucisson en brioche* and the ballottine of pheasant and the ox-cheek salad it was difficult to choose.

Gnafron's Apron

I decided to go on to her great speciality *le Tablier de Gnafron* or Gnafron's Apron. It's tripe, cut in big squares and dipped in egg and breadcrumbs and fried and looking rather like *schnitzel*. This is served piping hot on extremely hot plates which are brought to table wrapped in white damask dinner napkins to keep them warm. It gets its curious name from one of the puppets in the French Punch and Judy show – Gnafron, a cobbler who is a greedy comic character who always wears a leather cobbler's apron. He was a great friend of little Guignol – the French Punch, adored tripe and was supposed to be a native of Lyon. You can see both of them in the marionette museum on the other side of the river.

You need best quality cooked tripe for this ancient delicious dish. Cut it in largish triangles like a doll's apron. Dip them in egg beaten up with salt, pepper, a little grated lemon rind and one extra egg yolk. Then roll the pieces in a mixture of soft, white breadcrumbs and crushed, unsweetened rusks (what the French call *biscottes*). Heat some oil in a frying pan and then put in your six tripe "aprons" letting them brown and cook gently for 10 minutes. Take them out of the pan all golden crunchy. Put them in a dish in a warm oven while you make the sauce.

Cold Sauce for Hot Tripe or Chicken

This is served cold with the very hot tripe "aprons" and some plainly boiled potatoes, and is rather like a mayonnaise. Put 125 ml (¼-pint) dry, white wine in a little pan with 2 finely chopped shallots and let it simmer till reduced by about half. Then cool it. Get a pudding basin and in it beat up 1 egg yolk, 1 dessertspoon of French mustard and a little salt and pepper, with a wooden spoon. Pour 250 ml (½-pint) of olive oil into a jug. Add it to the egg mixture beating all the time, very slowly, *drop by drop* at first till the sauce begins to thicken. Then go faster gradually trickling the oil into the mixture as you beat it. If you go too fast it curdles, and you would then have to begin again, beating up another plain egg yolk and gradually beating in the original mixture. When the sauce has taken and thickened, add the shallots and white wine, and if liked, just before serving, a little chopped tarragon. The sauce is also very good with hot, fried, egged and crumbed chicken, or even with fish.

It made a delicious dish which I thoroughly enjoyed, though my companion more cautiously had roasted guinea fowl done with bacon and grapes and we had a half litre carafe of Chiroubles rouge with our supper, a wine *qui a de l'amour* as they say locally.

Though Madame Léa Bidaut's restaurant is less formal and somewhat cheaper than the three-star restaurants in the Guide Michelin, it is just as famous. She has been running it for the last 25 years and the regulars all say it is one of the best bistros in Lyon.

Hot Baked Pike

Another of the great specialities of the City of Lyon is hot baked pike, a delicious recipe which would be almost as good with a whole fresh haddock weighing about 800 g (2 lb). Dip it first in a little milk, about 3 tablespoons, then in about 2 tablespoons of seasoned flour. Brown it on either side in a frying pan in 100 g (4 oz) of hot frothing butter. Reduce the heat and continue cooking for 10 minutes, then lay it in an ovenproof dish. Meanwhile, having roughly chopped 200 g ($\frac{1}{2}$-lb) of button mushrooms lay them round the fish. Sprinkle both with chopped parsley, salt and pepper. Bring two glasses of white wine to the boil in the buttery frying pan in which you cooked the fish. Pour it over the fish and bake it in a very hot oven (230°C, 450°F, Mark 8) for about 20 minutes.

What's Cooking in the Casserole

Have you an old brown casserole? There are some marvellous earthy casserole dishes especially designed for long slow cooking which snuggle into the oven and sit there as long as you like, bubbling with delight. Even the cheapest cuts of beef, shin or leg, flank, brisket and even ox-heart, become deliciously tender and are full of flavour if one fries them first and then cooks them very slowly in a fireproof dish with a lid on. Cook them all night, or all day if you are out at work, in the very lowest heat of the oven. I once left an earthenware pot of ox-cheek for 36 hours on top of the stove that heats the bath water. The stove was never hot enough to boil the contents of the pot but at the end of 36 hours the ox-cheek was tender enough to cut with a spoon.

All one needs is a fireproof casserole with a well-fitting lid, good-looking enough to come straight to table. They come in everything from fireproof glass to cast iron or French flowerpot pottery, but I have always thought the food tastes better in the brown earthenware ones, just as tea always seems to be better out of an old brown teapot.

Casseroled Beef

Leave the meat in one piece, brown it all over in fat with sliced onions. Put it in the pot with salt, pepper and only 1½ tablespoons of water. Tie some foil or greaseproof paper over the top, put the lid on and leave it for at least 4 hours in a fairly slow oven (170°C, 325°F, Mark 3). It will wait patiently for hours without coming to any harm. So will jacket potatoes which you can serve with it. Or it can be done very slowly on top of the stove with an asbestos mat under the pan. Just let it simmer for 3–4 hours on a low heat by which time the meat should be tender enough to cut with a spoon.

With Tomato

There are several versions of this luscious dish. You can brown your piece of brisket or stewing steak, 600–800 g (1½–2 lb) for four people, with 400 g (1 lb) of sliced onions. Add salt, pepper, mixed herbs and a small tin of those Italian tomatoes, not the tomato purée, and cook it slowly as usual. Add no other liquid.

With an Unctuous Gravy

For a dish with a really smooth gravy which will set in a jelly when cold, add 1–2 unsalted pig's trotters. I generally add chopped fried celery, carrot and onion with herbs and seasoning. This time you need 375 ml (¾-pint) of hot water. Let it simmer as usual. This is very good hot with its really tacky gravy. But if you skim all the fat off, the meat will also be quite delicious cold in its own jelly.

Navarin

One can also use the casserole for the delicious peasant stew or *navarin* which is sometimes served in south-west France with a very good claret. You want about 800 g (2 lb) of stewing lamb, middle neck cutlets would be very good. Put them in a casserole, brown them in lard or dripping with two large chopped cloves of garlic. Sprinkle a spoonful of flour on top and let this brown, stirring gently. Add a pinch of mixed herbs, salt and pepper, hot water to cover and a small tin of tomato purée. Let it all simmer for about an hour or until tender. Peel and chop 4 small onions, 4 carrots, a bit of celery and some turnip. Brown these in a little pan and put them to cook in your casserole half an hour before serving, with 3 or 4 potatoes cut in chunks. Taste for seasoning, skim off any surplus fat and there it is – delicious!

Pork and Butter Beans

Pork and butter beans is another good heart-warming family dish of which I am very fond. Pour some hot water over 300 g (12 oz) of dried butter beans (or of lentils or split peas, if you like) and leave them about 3 hours to soak. Then, having bought a little bacon joint, put it in a pan of cold water, bring this slowly to the boil. Drain both beans and bacon and put them in your fireproof casserole with a large chopped onion, 2 chopped carrots, a pig's trotter and, if you have any, a bit of turnip and some celery. Add a tin of peeled tomatoes, 375 ml (¾-pint) of water, some pepper and mixed herbs. Cover your casserole closely as for the pot roast and cook it for 2–2½ hours in a fairly slow oven (170°C, 325°F, Mark 3), or for 4–5 hours on a slightly lower temperature. Then brown a sliced onion in a little fat, stir in a dessertspoon of flour and brown this too before stirring both into the main dish just before serving. Add the contents of a well-drained tin of frankfurter sausages at the same time for a really substantial dish.

Caution—Omelette Ahead!

I had been trying all week to resurrect an omelette. Hoping that at sun up on one particular morning the village of Les Andrieux, high up a steep and narrow Alpine valley somewhere south of Grenoble, would be making their traditional omelette once more for the first time in a hundred years.

The unfortunate villagers, who are deprived of the sun for a hundred days in winter, always used to celebrate its return on the 10th February. As soon as the night had gone, four shepherds from the hamlet announced the festivities with fife and trumpets warning the villagers to come out into the sun and make their omelette. But the whole ceremony had been virtually forgotten till I found an account of it in an old cookery book in the London Library. Nobody had ever heard of it nor knew where it was. The book said the village was in Switzerland but when I contacted the Swiss they told me, after some research, there was no such place anywhere in Switzerland. "Try the French Alps," they said.

At first nobody in France could find it either for it turns out that even the name of the village has been changed since the book was written, but at last I had it. It is now combined with another village making 300 people altogether and called La Chapelle en Valgaudemar, a tiny place nearly 4,000 feet up a very narrow, snow-blocked valley just off the route taken by Napoleon when he escaped from Elba and marched triumphantly on Paris. It seems that this is a very old custom going back into the mists of time and that it is fully described in the departmental records for the year 1808.

The parish priest – Monsieur le Curé – was quite delightful. "It is quite true," he said, "there was a custom every year when the sun came back to make an omelette on the bridge over the river where the sun first touched the valley. It is now called the *Pont d'Omelette*. There are, perhaps, people alive who still remember this omelette, it isn't made now." He told me that it was a very pretty, quite charming ceremony and was done towards 10 o'clock in the morning when the sun first touches the bridge of the valley. "We tried to revive it about 15 years ago but everyone in the village was very disappointed and although it was pretty, no one wants to go on with it now. I am very moved," said Monsieur le Curé, "that you should know of our omelette in London."

I decided that something must be done about it and spent weary hours screaming *'allo, 'allo, ne quittez pas on va vous parler* down telephone receivers where a hundred people seemed to be frying chips. With all the resources of the *Daily Express* behind me I went into action, so did the Paris office. Monsieur Hulot would have loved it. There are only about ten telephones in the village, most of them public call boxes. There is no *gendarme* either and the mayor – whose permission is *obviously* essential before making an omelette on the public highway – is not on the telephone. Finally we got on to the Post Office, the kind of place that if you have been on holiday in France you must remember well, but anyway the postman promised to bring *Monsieur le Maire* to the telephone. This, I said to myself, is the old unchanged rural France which is as it was in the days of Napoleon, or Clochemerle for that matter.

"*Ah non,*" said Monsieur Lucien Mazet, the mayor, "it cannot be done so fast." He thinks my idea of resurrecting the omelette is charming but we cannot do it this year. There would be all the omelette forms to fill in for lighting the fire on the bridge. He himself would be the only person responsible enough to cook it. After discussing it, so to speak, with his *chef de cabinet*, the postman, and other men of the village, he thinks there is no time for all the preparations.

"When it is done, Madame, it must be in a proper manner with full pomp and ceremony." Madame Cacealn the *patronne* of the local café was equally firm and said it would not be right for her to go out into the snow and fry it. "I think the mayor, Monsieur Mazet, could do it properly," she said, "besides I am not really of the village for I live four kilometres off." It is nice to know that some things are unchanged. *Vive la France!*

Here, anyway, is the recipe for the famous omelette.

Les Andrieux Omelette

It is quite easy, and is made with cheese and bacon and has fried bread in it. For 4–6 people beat up 8 eggs in a terrine or big basin with half a glass of milk and 100 g (4 oz) of grated cheese – Gruyère is best but Cheddar would do. Add some pepper but not too much salt because of the flavour of the bacon in it. Dice 125 g (5 oz) of smoked bacon or raw ham and dice some white bread. Fry both gently in a pan with about 25 g (1 oz) of butter. Fish out the bits of bread when they are crisp and golden, then tip the egg mixture into the pan with the bacon pieces and hot butter. Margarine is no good here – it sometimes makes an omelette stick. Stir the eggs a bit at first, very gently, then as the bottom part goes solid wrinkle it up. Push it very gently towards the middle with a fork or wooden spoon so it all heaps up like a rumpled unmade bed and more of the liquid runs down into the pan. Scatter the diced fried bread on top, fold it over while still runny, slide it onto a plate and serve at once. If liked, and if you have only a small frying pan, make two omelettes, dividing the mixture in half, and then starting again when the first one is cooked.

An Alpine Omelette

Large, flat, unfolded peasant omelettes are popular too in the French and Swiss Alps.

Peel, dice and fry some potatoes gently in butter with a lid on the pan, stir them occasionally, adding salt when they are light brown and crunchy. Beat up 4 eggs with salt, pepper, a couple of spoonfuls grated cheese and a tablespoon of cream. Pour this over the potatoes. Stir for a moment with a fork until it is like very wet scrambled eggs, then let it go solid. Brown the top under the grill and slide the omelette out whole onto a hot plate.

In some villages, peeled, finely sliced onions are fried with the potatoes, and in other mountain valleys it is made without any potatoes at all. The onions are fried gently until they are soft and golden, then mixed with grated cheese, and the seasoned beaten eggs and cream are poured on top. It is then cooked as before.

My Favourite Foods

When all is said and done, bought and sold, eaten and washed up, all the recipes have been tried and elaborate food discussed, there is a lot to be said for bacon and eggs. I think perhaps they are my favourite food, the one dish that I am always pleased to eat. This triumph of the British kitchen has gone round the world and perhaps contributed as much to the delight of nations as that other British invention, football.

I have a lot of ancient and leather-bound cookery books in my study, some going back 300 years and more. Two of them were used by chefs who cooked not only for Queen Anne but King Charles II. I can, however, find no reference to *bacon and eggs* earlier than about 1850. Was it too simple to put on paper? Had nobody thought of it? The 19th-century recipes seem to be for ham and eggs – cold boiled ham with an egg on top, horrible to my mind.

I was once given something of the sort on a Greek night flight which touched down at Athens on its way to Cyprus. Half asleep I was presented at 6 a.m. with a tray of hot coffee and so called " bacon and eggs". What was it? Cold boiled ham with poached eggs *warmed in dark green olive oil.* I could not eat it.

Bacon and eggs are obviously no more foolproof than that other great invention of ours, liver and bacon.

My other two favourite foods that I can eat at almost any time are more foreign. One is just a hot soup plate full of plain boiled steaming spaghetti, the long kind from a packet, just with a lot of melted butter and grated cheese on top. Dead simple but the kind of comfortable food I like when I come home too tired to cook anything much.

The third dish is kidneys with mustard, *rognons sautées à la moutarde* they call it in French. I have sought them out on menus and ordered them in little restaurants all over France when I should, perhaps, have been trying the chef's special dish so as to report about it in the *Daily Express*. I think they are delicious. On the Continent people generally use calves' kidneys for such recipes, but we eat very little veal here and the few kidneys there are seem to be sold to restaurants; but ox kidney, if fairly light in colour and not too tough, can be used instead. Ask the butcher if he thinks they are tender. Get him to leave the kidney in one piece, slice it yourself at home (don't chop it in chunks) and take out the centre core and stringy bits of fat. You will need a whole ox kidney or most of it. Pig's kidneys are also very good when cooked like this. Allow two each and slice them in half on the plump side without quite cutting them in two.

Kidneys with Mustard

Fry the kidneys in butter and oil adding 100 g (4 oz) of sliced mushrooms, then stir about a dessertspoon of French mustard into the buttery juices round the kidneys. Put them on a hot plate with the mushrooms while you add 3 tablespoons of cream or very thick top of the milk to the juices in the pan. Stir it, scraping up the delicious bits in the bottom. Pour this over the kidneys and mushrooms. Eat it at once with hunks of bread to mop up the gravy. Do not add salt till after the kidneys are cooked, it makes them tough.

Kidney Kebabs

Kidneys, bacon and mushrooms together will also make excellent and fairly inexpensive kebabs for six people. You will need 150 g (6 oz) mushrooms, two or three rashers of streaky bacon and 6 lambs' kidneys. Cut the bacon, kidney and mushrooms in pieces of a suitable size. Then thread them alternately on six skewers. Thread bay leaves on to the skewers here and there between the pieces of meat. These smell delicious when grilling and give a subtle flavour to the whole thing. Some people also add small pieces of liver together with the mushrooms and kidneys. Roll the loaded skewers in cooking oil, season them with a little salt and some pepper, grill them for about 15 minutes. Turn them from time to time so they cook evenly all round, but hold the ends of the skewers in a cloth or oven cloth so you do not burn your fingers. Put them on a hot dish with garlic butter on top.

Garlic Butter

This is simply butter mashed with chopped garlic, chopped parsley and a little pepper. Put the dish in a warm oven for a few minutes so the butter melts, but not to cook the kebabs any further. We have a tossed salad with them. They are almost as good as bacon and eggs.

Index